Introduction

The Art of Living as Ritual

"Ritual is how we return home — to the body, the breath, and the sacred rhythm of our own life."

In a world that moves too quickly, we often forget the quiet beauty of being.

The TrueJoy Living Ritual Book is an invitation to slow down and remember.

It is not a book to be read once — it's a companion to be lived with.

Each page is a gentle reminder that healing doesn't happen in grand gestures, but in the small, consistent moments we choose to make sacred.

When you light a candle with intention, breathe before you speak, or sip your tea in gratitude — you are practicing ritual. You are transforming the ordinary into something holy.

This is **not** about perfection.
It's about presence.
It's about coming home to yourself again and again, until that feeling of wholeness no longer feels like a moment — but a way of being.

Your life is the ceremony ~ Your breath is the prayer ~Your presence is the ritual.

Welcome home — to your TrueJoy.

~ Joy Hafner
Founder of TrueJoy Living

Quieting the Mind

Intention

Overthinking is the mind's way of trying to feel safe — it believes
if it can control everything, it can prevent pain.
But real safety doesn't come from control; it comes from trust.
Today's ritual invites you to step out of the storm of thoughts and
return to the quiet soil of the present moment.
"I release the need to figure it all out."

Mantra of the Ritual

"I trust the pause. In stillness, clarity finds me."

Optional Enhancements

Before bed, apply Focus Balm (lavender + frankincense)
to the temples and soles of feet. Keep a smooth stone or piece of
onyx on your desk to touch when mental noise rises.
Pair with Rooted Bath Soak at the end of a long thinking day to
anchor thoughts back to the body.

Science Meets Soul

Overthinking activates the brain's default mode network —
the same system that calms when we ground, breathe, or
move with awareness. Grounding shifts the body from mental
loops to present awareness, allowing intuition and creativity to surface.
Stillness is not the absence of thought; it's the spaciousness between them.

Returning to Simplicity

The Ritual: From Thought to Stillness

1. Light for Clarity

Light your TrueJoy Clarity Candle (sage + eucalyptus + lemon).
As the scent rises, imagine a gentle wind clearing fog from your mind.
Whisper: "My thoughts are clouds passing through the sky of my awareness."

Healing Note: Lemon and eucalyptus oils are known in aromatherapy to activate the prefrontal cortex —
improving focus while calming overstimulation.

2. Anoint the Mind

Rub 1–2 drops of TrueJoy Clarity Oil (rosemary + sandalwood + basil) between your palms.
Place your hands lightly on your temples, then the back of your neck.
Feel warmth spreading through the mind's edges.
Repeat: "I am not my thoughts. I am the awareness beneath them."

Ancient Wisdom: In traditional Ayurvedic marma therapy, temple touch releases pitta (mental heat) —
soothing worry and obsessive thinking.

Returning to Simplicity
The Ritual: From Thought to Stillness

3. Breathe the Reset

Sit comfortably, feet grounded.
Inhale through your nose for 4 counts, hold for 2, exhale slowly for 8.
On each exhale, visualize thoughts dissolving like mist.
Continue for 5 rounds.

Product Companion: Mist Peace Aura Spray (lavender + ylang-ylang + bergamot) between each breath.
Why it works: Longer exhalations activate the vagus nerve, shifting the nervous system into rest-and-digest mode.

4. Hand-to-Heart Awareness

Gently place one hand over your heart, the other over your belly.
Ask inwardly:
"What's really asking for my attention right now?"
Listen.
You don't need to answer — just witness.

Healing Note: Overthinking quiets when we move from mental loops to body presence.

5. Seal the Stillness

Close your ritual by journaling a simple phrase:
"What if I didn't have to know right now?"
Blow out the candle, symbolizing release of the need to control.

Journaling

(Use this space to write, draw, or simply breathe into the lessons of today's ritual. There is no right or wrong — only what your soul needs to express.)

Soothing the Storm

Intention

Emotional waves are not signs of weakness — they are energy asking to move.
When we fight them, they flood us. When we ground
and breathe, they flow through.
This ritual helps you be with what feels big — not to fix it,
but to feel safe inside it.
It brings your awareness out of the storm of emotion and into the
calm soil of the body.
"Even when emotions rise, I am steady at my roots."

Mantra of the Ritual

*"I am the still point beneath the waves.
I am safe to feel. I am safe to release."*

Optional Enhancements

Journal one sentence beginning with: "My emotions are trying to tell me..."
Place a smoky quartz or black tourmaline stone beside your
bath or on your nightstand.
End with gentle humming — vibration regulates the vagus nerve,
deepening calm.

Healing Integration

Emotional overwhelm happens when the body can't discharge excess energy.
Grounding through breath, scent, and touch reminds your system
how to complete the stress cycle — transforming chaos into calm,
tears into release, and emotion into wisdom.
"Grounding doesn't erase the storm. It teaches you how to stand in the rain."

Returning to Stillness

The Ritual: From Flood to Flow

1. Create a Safe Container

Light your TrueJoy Sacred Earth Candle (vetiver + amber + vanilla).
Sit comfortably, feet touching the floor or the ground.
Imagine a circle of warm golden light surrounding you — your emotional sanctuary.
Whisper: "Only calm and compassion belong here."

Healing Note: Creating a ritual boundary tells the nervous system, "You are safe to feel."

2. Apply Calm Through Touch

Warm a few drops of TrueJoy Calm Body Oil (chamomile + sandalwood + sweet orange)
between your palms. Slowly press your hands over your heart, shoulders, and
stomach — wherever tension gathers.
As you exhale, soften the space under your palms.
Say softly: "I hold myself with tenderness."

Science Meets Soul: Physical touch releases oxytocin, the hormone of safety and connection, soothing emotional intensity.

3. Breathe Through the Waves

Inhale through your nose for 4 counts
Hold gently for 2 counts
Exhale through your mouth for 8 counts — as if sighing out heavy energy
On each breath, visualize releasing dense emotion down your body into the Earth.
Continue for 2–3 minutes.

Product Companion: Mist your space with Peace Aura Spray (lavender + ylang-ylang + bergamot) before beginning.
Ancient Wisdom: Indigenous and Taoist traditions teach that the Earth transforms heavy energy — it never rejects it. Your emotions are compost for new calm.

4. Ground the Emotion Physically

Place both hands flat on your thighs or on the floor.
Feel the texture, the weight, the steadiness beneath you.
Imagine your emotions as waves meeting rock — energy that moves but does not harm.

Mantra: "I can feel deeply and remain steady."

5. Release & Restore

If tears come, let them.
When ready, fill your bathtub with warm water and add TrueJoy Rooted Bath Soak (Epsom salt + ginger + rose petals).
As you submerge, visualize every cell being rewoven with peace.

"My body remembers calm."

Journaling

(Use this space to write, draw, or simply breathe into the lessons of today's ritual. There is no right or wrong — only what your soul needs to express.)

Reclaiming Inner Security Through Presence and Compassion

Intention

True safety begins when we learn to keep promises to ourselves —
not through perfection, but through consistency.
This ritual is a soft return to the self: a remembering that you can be
your own safe place. Through scent, affirmation, and touch, it rewires the body
to associate self-attention with comfort, not criticism.

"I can trust myself to hold me."

Mantra of the Ritual

*"I am my own safe place.
My consistency creates my calm."*

Optional Enhancements

Place your hand on your heart whenever you notice self-doubt rising.
End your day with a single line in your journal: "I kept my word to myself today by…"
Pair this ritual weekly with Rooted Bath Soak to deepen embodiment and self-soothing.

Healing Integration

When you rebuild trust with yourself, the nervous system begins to relax —
no longer scanning for danger.
You learn that safety is not given by circumstances, but cultivated from within.

"Self-trust is not built in grand moments; it's built in every quiet promise you keep."

Reclaiming Inner Security Through Presence and Compassion

The Ritual: Coming Home to Yourself

1. Light the Sacred Earth

Light your TrueJoy Sacred Earth Candle (amber + vetiver + vanilla).
Watch the flame and imagine it igniting a warm glow inside your heart.
Whisper: *"I am safe within this light."*

Healing Note: Steady flame-gazing slows brain-wave patterns and anchors attention in the present —
the first step toward self-trust.

2. Anoint the Heart

Warm a few drops of TrueJoy Grounding Body Oil (patchouli + frankincense + sweet orange) in your palms.
Place both hands over your heart and feel its rhythm.
Say softly: "I honor this heartbeat — it has carried me through everything."
Breathe into the warmth until your body relaxes under your hands.

Science Meets Soul: Gentle self-touch calms the vagus nerve and signals to the brain: "I am cared for."

3. Affirm Trust Through Voice

Close your eyes and repeat slowly:
"I keep my word to myself."
"I follow through with kindness."
"I am patient with my becoming."
Let each statement sink into your body, not just your mind.

Why it works: Spoken affirmation activates the limbic system — helping belief feel real through tone and vibration.

Reclaiming Inner Security Through Presence and Compassion

The Ritual: Coming Home to Yourself

4. The Heart Balm Ritual

Take a small amount of TrueJoy Heart Balm (rose + neroli + cacao butter) and massage gently into the center of your
chest in slow circles.As you do, imagine layering safety over old self-doubt — like wrapping your heart in a soft shawl.

Say quietly: "I forgive myself for ever thinking I was unsafe in my own care."

*Ancient Wisdom: In Egyptian and Ayurvedic healing, anointing the heart was a sacred act of aligning spirit and body —
restoring emotional equilibrium.*

5. Seal the Trust

Write in your journal:
"One way I can show up for myself this week is..."
Choose something small (drinking water, walking, setting a boundary).
Lightly mist your space with Peace Aura Spray (lavender + bergamot).
Sit for one minute in gratitude for your own presence. "I am learning to trust the one who never leaves — me."

Journaling

(Use this space to write, draw, or simply breathe into the lessons of today's ritual. There is no right or wrong — only what your soul needs to express.)

Finding Peace in the Flow of What Is

Intention

Control is a safety mechanism — the mind's attempt to manage
the unknown. But control tightens what trust softens.
This ritual helps you return to the quiet rhythm beneath striving —
the rhythm that reminds you that everything unfolds in perfect time.

"I trust that what is meant for me will arrive when I am ready to receive it."

Mantra of the Ritual

*"I trust the timing of my life.
I am safe in the pause between what was and what will be."*

Optional Enhancements

Repeat this ritual under the New Moon for renewal and intention resetting.
Keep TrueJoy Calm Oil on your desk — inhale deeply before making big decisions.
Place a bowl of salt water at your bedside overnight to symbolically absorb residual
control energy; discard it in the morning.

Healing Integration

Control is an illusion created by fear; trust is the truth remembered through presence.
Grounding teaches that peace doesn't come from certainty —
it comes from alignment with the natural flow of life.

"The Earth never rushes, yet everything blooms in perfect time."

Finding Peace in the Flow of What Is

The Ritual: The Art of Surrender

1. Light the Surrender Flame

Light your TrueJoy Surrender Candle (cedarwood + sage + bergamot).
Watch the flame sway.
Whisper softly: "Even the flame moves with the air. I can, too."
Take three slow breaths, syncing with the candle's rhythm.

Healing Note: Cedarwood soothes the adrenals and quiets the "doing" brain, inviting the body into a state of surrender.

2. The Flow Breath

Sit or stand comfortably with both feet grounded. Inhale through your nose for 4 counts.
Exhale through your mouth for 6 counts. On each exhale, imagine the word "release."
On each inhale, imagine the word "receive." Repeat for 10 cycles, feeling your body soften into trust.

Why it works: Breath-work lengthens the parasympathetic response, calming the fear that drives control.

3. Anoint the Hands of Letting Go

Warm a few drops of TrueJoy Calm Oil (chamomile + sandalwood + clary sage) between your palms.
Rub your hands slowly together, then open them in front of your heart, palms up.
Whisper: "I let go of my grip on outcomes. I open to what's meant for me."

Ancient Wisdom: In Ayurveda, open-palm rituals were practiced to signal receptivity — a reminder that abundance flows to hands not clenched in fear.

4. The Flow Soak

Prepare a warm bath with TrueJoy Flow Salt Soak (Epsom salt + rose petals + geranium).
As you stir the water, say: "I dissolve resistance. I float with what is."
Step in and imagine each muscle relaxing, each thought loosening.
Let the water carry away the need to rush or push.

Optional: Keep the candle burning safely nearby as a symbol of surrender.

5. Journal the Letting Go

After your bath, write one sentence that begins:
"I release control over..."
and one that begins:
"I trust that..."
End with gratitude for one thing unfolding perfectly right now — even if it's small.

Healing Note: Writing out surrender shifts the subconscious from fear of the unknown to acceptance of flow.

Journaling

(Use this space to write, draw, or simply breathe into the lessons of today's ritual. There is no right or wrong — only what your soul needs to express.)

Becoming the Steady Center in Shifting Seasons

Intention

Uncertainty is uncomfortable because it reminds us we are not in control.
But within that discomfort lives possibility — and resilience.
This ritual helps you ground not through certainty, but through connection.
"Even as everything changes, I remain whole."

Mantra of the Ritual

*"The Earth beneath me never questions change.
I am rooted, I am steady, I am safe."*

Optional Enhancements

Place a small rock, crystal, or piece of driftwood in your pocket as a "stability talisman."
Walk barefoot outdoors for three minutes, noticing texture, sound, and temperature —
the language of the Earth.
Add this ritual to times of transition (moving homes, new job, endings, beginnings).

Healing Integration

Uncertainty will always exist — but anxiety about it doesn't have to.
Grounding teaches us that change is not chaos; it is movement within a greater pattern.
When we anchor to what is constant (our breath, our presence, the Earth), uncertainty transforms into openness.
"Roots do not fear the wind — they strengthen beneath it."

Becoming the Steady Center
in Shifting Seasons

The Ritual: Anchoring Amid Change

1. Light the Stability Flame

Light your TrueJoy Stability Candle (sandalwood + myrrh + cedar).
Watch the flame — steady, yet alive.
Whisper: "I am centered in this moment."
As the scent fills the space, let the body exhale deeply.

Healing Note: Sandalwood and cedar are grounding oils used in ancient temple rituals to symbolize unshakable presence.

2. Root Through the Body

Apply TrueJoy Root Oil (vetiver + patchouli + black pepper) to the soles of your feet.
As you massage it in, imagine roots extending from your feet deep into the Earth — dark, steady, strong.
Feel your weight supported by what does not move.
Whisper: "I am connected to something larger than this moment."

Science Meets Soul: The act of applying oil to the feet activates grounding reflex points and signals safety to the parasympathetic nervous system.

3. The Breath of Belonging

Sit or stand comfortably with both feet planted.
Inhale for 4 counts — imagine drawing strength from the Earth. Hold for 2 counts.
Exhale for 6 counts — release resistance to what's changing.
With every breath, feel your body anchored deeper into now.

Ancient Wisdom: In many indigenous traditions, "breathing with the Earth" was a sacred practice to exchange energy — receiving stability, releasing fear.

Becoming the Steady Center in Shifting Seasons

The Ritual: Anchoring Amid Change

4. The Earth Balm Touch

Take a small amount of TrueJoy Earth Balm (shea butter + cedarwood + frankincense) and warm it between your palms.
Place one hand on your heart, one on your belly.
Feel the rise and fall of breath — your body's natural rhythm, constant even as life shifts.
Say quietly: "Change moves around me, not through my core."

Healing Note: This touch brings awareness to your body's center — the energetic axis of balance
between heart (emotion) and gut (intuition).

5. Seal the Trust

Write in your journal:
"One thing I cannot control but can accept is..."
"One thing that remains steady within me is..."
End by misting TrueJoy Peace Aura Spray into the air, letting its scent signal completion.

Journaling

(Use this space to write, draw, or simply breathe into the lessons of today's ritual. There is no right or wrong — only what your soul needs to express.)

Rooting in Love When the Heart Feels Heavy

Intention

Grief is love with nowhere to go.
This ritual gives it a path — through your breath, your tears, your touch,
and your connection to the Earth.
You are not asked to let go of what you love, only to let love flow through you again.
"Even in loss, I am held."

Mantra of the Ritual

*"Even through tears, I am grounded in love.
What I release, I return to light."*

Optional Enhancements

Keep a small bowl of salt and petals near your candle — each time grief rises,
drop a petal in for remembrance Take a barefoot walk and imagine leaving footprints of release with every step.
End your evening with TrueJoy Lotus Milk Bath to soothe the heart chakra and restore peace before sleep.

Healing Integration

Grief doesn't end; it evolves. When we ground through grief, we honor both the ache and the beauty of love that remains. Each breath, each tear, becomes part of the healing soil from which new compassion grows.

"The Earth teaches us; nothing truly dies — it changes form and continues to give."

Becoming the Steady Center in Shifting Seasons

The Ritual: Returning Love to the Earth

1. Light the Comfort Flame

Light your TrueJoy Comfort Candle (rose + myrrh + sandalwood). Let the soft light and scent fill your space.
Whisper: "I light this flame for love that continues."
As you gaze at the flame, allow memories, emotions, or tears to surface freely.

Healing Note: Myrrh has been used in ancient burial and mourning rituals for thousands of years — symbolizing eternal love and transformation.

2. Anoint the Heart of Memory

Warm a small amount of TrueJoy Heart Balm (rose + neroli + cacao butter) in your palms.
Place both hands over your heart and close your eyes. Feel your heartbeat — steady, ancient, alive.
Whisper: "This heart still beats with love."

Ancient Wisdom: In Egyptian ritual, the heart was considered the seat of the soul — a vessel of both memory and eternity.

3. Breathe with the Earth

Sit with your feet firmly on the ground. Inhale slowly through your nose for 4 counts — imagine drawing calm up
from the Earth. Exhale through your mouth for 6 counts — imagine releasing sorrow back into the soil.
Continue for 7 rounds, letting the breath become a soft rhythm between grief and grace.

Science Meets Soul: Deep breathing engages the vagus nerve, helping release emotional tension stored in the chest.

4. The Release Mist Ritual

Mist your space with TrueJoy Release Mist (frankincense + lavender + bergamot).
As the mist falls, imagine your grief being blessed, not erased — transformed into light
Whisper: "I honor what was. I bless what remains."

Healing Note: Frankincense is known as the "oil of truth" — it opens the heart while soothing the nervous system.

5. Return to the Body

Wrap yourself in a soft blanket or shawl. Place one hand on your belly and one on your heart.
Feel the rise and fall — grief moves like waves, and you are the shore that holds them.
Sit quietly for a few minutes, breathing slowly, until your body begins to relax.
"The Earth holds what I cannot."

6. Closing the Circle

Blow out the candle, symbolizing peace returning to the heart. Write in your journal:
"Today, I loved by remembering…"

Journaling

(Use this space to write, draw, or simply breathe into the lessons of today's ritual.
There is no right or wrong — only what your soul needs to express.)

Releasing Tension

Intention

Conflict is inevitable, but suffering after it is optional.
Peace doesn't come from being right—it comes from returning to presence.
This ritual helps you clear the energetic residue of tension, soften defensiveness,
and ground back into love—first for yourself, then for others.

"I choose peace over pride, and calm over control."

Mantra of the Ritual

"I breathe in peace,
I release all tension.
I forgive, and I am free."

Optional Enhancements

Diffuse TrueJoy Harmony Candle scent during meditation or while journaling
after conflict. Take a short grounding walk to let the body discharge leftover
emotion through movement. Pair this ritual with a warm cup of chamomile
or tulsi tea to soothe the digestive and emotional centers.

Healing Integration

After conflict, our body holds stories the mind tries to move past.
Grounding through ritual teaches emotional completion—
the difference between "moving on" and actually releasing.
Peace becomes not a concept, but a felt sense of return.

"The Earth holds no grudges—it transforms everything it touches back into life."

Restoring Inner Harmony

The Ritual: Returning to Center

1. Light the Harmony Flame

Light your TrueJoy Harmony Candle (lavender + chamomile + sandalwood).
As it burns, close your eyes and take three slow breaths.
Whisper: "I release what was said. I keep only what brings wisdom."
Let the flame become a symbol of softening—your light remaining steady through the storm.

Healing Note: Lavender and sandalwood slow the heart rate and restore equilibrium to the emotional center.

2. Calm the Body Through Touch

Warm a few drops of TrueJoy Calm Body Oil (chamomile + clary sage + bergamot) between your palms.
Gently press your hands over your shoulders, then the back of your neck—places where conflict energy collects.
As you exhale, imagine tension leaving through your fingertips.
Say softly: "I release the weight of defense. My body remembers peace."

Science Meets Soul: Touch lowers cortisol, slows breathing, and helps the body shift from "fight" to "rest."

3. The Breath of Neutrality

Sit with your spine tall, both feet on the ground. Inhale through your nose for 4 counts.
Hold for 2. Exhale through your mouth for 8 counts.
On each exhale, visualize a soft gray light washing over your chest—neutralizing emotional charge.

Ancient Wisdom: In Zen breathing, neutrality is considered the state closest to peace—
where nothing is clung to or rejected.

4. Clear the Energy of the Room

Mist your surroundings with TrueJoy Peace Aura Spray (lavender + ylang-ylang + bergamot).As you
walk through your space, whisper: "I clear this space of anger, resentment, and fear.
I invite calm, compassion, and understanding."
Why it works: The act of clearing a space helps your nervous system signal completion—
the conflict is over, safety has returned.

5. Forgive, Then Release

Sit quietly and place one hand on your heart, one on your belly.
Repeat: "I forgive myself for reacting. I forgive them for not knowing better.
I allow peace to take root again."
Feel your heartbeat steady as your breath deepens.
Healing Note: Forgiveness is a nervous system regulation tool—
it releases the body from holding the stress of the story.

6. Seal in Harmony

Blow out the candle, symbolizing completion and closure. Write in your journal:
"What part of me felt unsafe in that moment? What truth did I learn from this?"
Mist yourself once more with Peace Aura Spray, imagining a gentle cocoon of light surrounding you.
"I am at peace with myself. I am free."

Journaling

(Use this space to write, draw, or simply breathe into the lessons of today's ritual. There is no right or wrong — only what your soul needs to express.)

Opening the Mind

Intention

Your intuition is not a mystery — it's your body's language of wisdom.
When you slow down and listen, you discover that your inner knowing is always speaking.
This ritual helps you tune into that frequency with clarity, compassion, and trust.

"The answers I seek are already within me."

Mantra of the Ritual

"I am guided.
I am clear.
I trust my inner wisdom."

Optional Enhancements

Practice this ritual during moonlight or before sleep for dream guidance.
Pair with journaling prompts like: "When does my intuition feel strongest? What happens when I ignore it?"
Keep a small amethyst or lapis lazuli stone on your altar to enhance clarity.

Healing Integration

When you learn to listen inwardly, you stop searching outwardly.
Intuition is the bridge between the grounded self and the infinite self — the meeting point of Earth and Spirit.
This ritual builds confidence in that quiet voice that already knows the way.

"The more I trust my inner light, the brighter my path becomes."

Listening with the Heart

The Ritual: Listening Beyond the Noise

1. Light the Insight Flame

Light your TrueJoy Insight Candle (lavender + clary sage + sandalwood). As it burns, take three slow breaths.
Whisper: "I open my mind and heart to higher knowing."
Allow the scent to fill the air — soft, steady, and clear.

*Healing Note: Clary sage has long been used to open intuition and balance the third eye chakra,
while sandalwood calms the analytical mind.*

2. Anoint the Third Eye

Place one drop of TrueJoy Third Eye Oil (frankincense + blue lotus + rosemary) on your fingertip.
Gently touch the space between your eyebrows. Close your eyes and feel the cooling sensation.
Whisper: "I see with wisdom. I trust my vision."

*Ancient Wisdom: In Egyptian and Vedic traditions, oils and resins were used to activate the pineal gland —
considered the energetic "eye of the soul."*

3. The Breath of Clarity

Inhale through your nose for 4 counts. Hold for 2. Exhale slowly through your mouth for 6 counts.
With every inhale, imagine breathing in light. With every exhale, release confusion or doubt.
Continue for 7 rounds, until your inner space feels still.

*Science Meets Soul: Focused breath-work increases oxygen flow to the prefrontal cortex —
enhancing intuition and calm decision-making.*

4. Stillness & Inner Listening

Sit quietly with your candle still burning.
Place one hand over your heart and one on your belly.
Ask inwardly: "What do I need to know right now?"
Don't force an answer — let it rise naturally as a feeling, image, or phrase.
Write any sensations or messages that come into your journal.

*Healing Note: Intuition often speaks in sensation before words —
goosebumps, warmth, or peace are its language.*

5. Mist to Integrate

Close your ritual by misting TrueJoy Calm Mist (lavender + chamomile + neroli) above your crown.
Inhale deeply.
Whisper: "I trust what I feel. I move with knowing."

Journaling

(Use this space to write, draw, or simply breathe into the lessons of today's ritual. There is no right or wrong — only what your soul needs to express.)

Opening the Channel to Express Your Inner Light

Intention

Creativity is the soul's way of playing in the physical world.
When we overthink, inspiration tightens; when we open, it flows.
This ritual reconnects you with your inner muse — the part of you that doesn't force, but allows.
"I am a vessel for creative flow."

Mantra of the Ritual

"I am open.
I am inspired.
I am the artist of my own life."

Optional Enhancements

Do this ritual with soft instrumental music or ambient nature sounds.
Burn a stick of palo santo before beginning to clear creative blocks.
Pair with a walk in nature — movement often sparks inspiration more than stillness.

Healing Integration

Creativity is your natural state — it's how your soul breathes.
When you create from grounding instead of striving, expression becomes effortless.
This ritual reminds you that inspiration doesn't need to be found; it's waiting to be felt.
"When I stop chasing ideas, they find me."

Opening the Channel to Express Your Inner Light

The Ritual: Opening the Creative Current

1. Light the Muse Flame

Light your TrueJoy Muse Candle (orange blossom + bergamot + vanilla).
Watch the flickering light as you breathe deeply. Whisper: "I open to the magic of creation."
Let the warm, citrus scent remind you that joy is your natural fuel.

Healing Note: Bergamot elevates mood and opens the solar plexus — the center of confidence and creative drive.

2. Awaken the Body

Stand tall and roll your shoulders back.
Begin gentle, free-flowing movement — stretching, swaying, or dancing softly.
Let your body move how it wants — no structure, no judgment.
As you move, repeat: "I release resistance. I move with flow."

Ancient Wisdom: In many traditions, creative inspiration was linked to movement — dance and rhythm were seen as gateways to divine creation.

3. Anoint with Flow Oil

Rub a few drops of TrueJoy Flow Oil (ylang-ylang + grapefruit + clary sage) on your wrists and over your heart.
Inhale the scent deeply, feeling your chest expand.
Say softly: "Inspiration flows through me with ease."

Science Meets Soul: Clary sage regulates serotonin levels and relieves creative tension by calming the limbic system.

4. Creative Breathwork

Sit or stand comfortably.
Inhale through your nose for 4 counts — imagine breathing in color and light.
Hold for 2.
Exhale through your mouth for 6 — releasing self-doubt.
After 5 rounds, pause in stillness and ask: "What wants to express through me today?"

Healing Note: Creative energy thrives in the pause — that breath between doing and being.

5. Creative Journaling or Expression

Take 10 minutes to journal, paint, doodle, or write freely — without editing.
Let your intuition lead, not logic.
Don't analyze; simply create.
When finished, mist TrueJoy Creative Mist (orange + peppermint + jasmine) above your workspace and say:

"This moment is my masterpiece."

Journaling

(Use this space to write, draw, or simply breathe into the lessons of today's ritual. There is no right or wrong — only what your soul needs to express.)

Awakening the Senses to Experience Life Fully

Intention

Presence is not about stillness — it's about aliveness.
This ritual reconnects you with your five senses as portals into the moment.
When you learn to experience the world through your senses instead of your thoughts, you rediscover beauty in the simplest details.

"I awaken to the miracle of this moment."

Mantra of the Ritual

"Through my senses, I awaken.
Through presence, I become whole."

Optional Enhancements

Play soft ambient or nature sounds during the ritual to deepen sensory experience.
Incorporate this ritual into your morning tea, meal, or skincare routine — turning daily acts into mindful meditation.
Use TrueJoy Senses Oil as daily perfume to remind yourself to return to now.

Healing Integration

Your senses are sacred messengers — they tether you to the here and now.
When awakened, they transform ordinary life into a living ceremony.
Through this ritual, you learn that mindfulness isn't stillness — it's participation.

"Presence is not found by leaving the world, but by feeling it fully."

Awakening the Senses to Experience Life Fully

The Ritual: Reclaiming Sensory Presence

1. Light the Presence Flame

Light your TrueJoy Presence Candle (amber + sandalwood + vanilla). Watch the flickering light as it dances. Whisper: "I open my senses to life." Inhale the scent and notice how warmth feels against your skin.

Healing Note: The combination of warm woods and sweet vanilla activates grounding and pleasure centers —

reminding the nervous system that safety can feel good.

2. The Five-Sense Awakening

Move through each sense slowly and intentionally:

Sight: Gaze softly at your surroundings. Notice colors, shadows, shapes. Ask: *"What beauty is here that I've never noticed before?"*

Sound: Close your eyes. Listen for layers of sound — distant, near, rhythmic. Whisper: *"I hear life all around me."*

Smell: Mist your space with TrueJoy Awaken Mist (citrus + rosemary + jasmine). Inhale deeply, letting scent become a doorway to presence.

Touch: Apply TrueJoy Senses Oil (ylang-ylang + sandalwood + rose) to your hands. Feel the texture, temperature, and softness as you rub your palms together. Place one hand on your heart, one on your belly, and breathe.

Taste Take a sip of water or herbal tea. Let it linger on your tongue. Feel gratitude for nourishment in its simplest form.

3. Stillness of the Senses

Sit quietly and let your senses integrate. Feel how awareness has expanded, how time feels slower. Whisper: "This moment is enough."

Science Meets Soul: Sensory mindfulness lowers cortisol and increases serotonin — teaching the body that presence equals peace.

4. Seal the Senses

Blow out your candle slowly, watching the smoke swirl and disappear. Whisper: "I carry this awareness into all I do." Smile softly — that is the face of presence.

Journaling

(Use this space to write, draw, or simply breathe into the lessons of today's ritual. There is no right or wrong — only what your soul needs to express.)

Awakening Emotional Presence

Intention

Love is the frequency of awakening.
This ritual helps you drop from your mind into your heart — the bridge
between spirit and humanity.
By opening the heart, you not only feel more connected to others, but more
at peace within yourself.

"My heart is open, radiant, and kind."

Mantra of the Ritual

"I love deeply,
I give gently,
I receive freely."

Optional Enhancements

Perform this ritual before connecting with loved ones or as a self-soothing
practice after emotional challenges.
Pair with soft rose quartz or green aventurine to amplify heart energy.
Play gentle harp or piano music to create a nurturing vibration.

Healing Integration

Opening the heart is an act of courage — it's choosing love over fear, softness
over defense. When the heart awakens, life begins to meet you halfway.
Through this ritual, love becomes not something to seek, but something
to embody.

"The more I open my heart, the more beauty I see."

Inner Warmth

The Ritual: Opening to Love and Compassion

1. Light the Love Flame

Light your TrueJoy Love Candle (rose + vanilla + sandalwood). Watch the flame glow warmly.
Whisper: "I open my heart to love, within and around me."
Inhale deeply — let the soft floral sweetness fill your chest.

Healing Note: Rose vibrates with the highest emotional frequency in aromatherapy —
opening compassion and dissolving heaviness.

2. Anoint the Heart

Warm a few drops of TrueJoy Heart Oil (rose + geranium + bergamot) between your palms.
Place your hands over your heart center. Take three deep breaths and whisper:
"It is safe to feel. It is safe to love."

Ancient Wisdom: In Ayurveda, rose was used to cool emotional heat and balance pitta dosha —
reminding the body that softness is strength.

3. Breath of Compassion

Inhale deeply through your nose, imagining soft pink light filling your chest.
Exhale slowly through your mouth, sending that light outward. Repeat for 7 rounds.
On each inhale, say silently: "May I be at peace." On each exhale, say: "May others be at peace."

Science Meets Soul: Compassion breath regulates the vagus nerve, enhancing empathy and connection
while calming emotional distress.

4. Mirror of Love

Sit before a mirror or reflective surface. Look into your own eyes.
Whisper softly: "You are enough. You are worthy of love. You are doing beautifully."
Place your hand on your heart and smile at your reflection.

Healing Note: Self-compassion reprograms the nervous system to associate vulnerability with safety —
unlocking emotional freedom.

5. Mist for Harmony

Mist TrueJoy Harmony Spray (lavender + ylang-ylang + sweet orange) over your chest or space.
Whisper: "Love flows freely through me."
Feel warmth spread through your body — calm, grounded, open.

6. Close with Gratitude

Blow out your candle and watch the smoke rise. Whisper:
"I release all that blocks love. I am open to receive and give with grace."
Sit quietly for a few moments in gratitude — for your heart, your breath, your tenderness.

Journaling

(Use this space to write, draw, or simply breathe into the lessons of today's ritual. There is no right or wrong — only what your soul needs to express.)

Reconnecting to Inner Lightness

Intention

Joy is sacred.
It's not about denial or distraction — it's about remembering that delight
is a form of devotion. This ritual invites you to return to your natural state
of wonder, curiosity, and ease — where every breath feels like a celebration.

"I awaken joy by allowing myself to play."

Mantra of the Ritual

"I choose joy.
I embody light.
I am free to play."

Optional Enhancements

Add laughter yoga, drumming, or free dancing.
Wear something colorful — let your outer world match your inner brightness.
Invite a friend or loved one to join — joy multiplies when shared.

Healing Integration

Joy is your birthright.
It doesn't require a reason — it's your natural vibration when you return to flow.
Through this ritual, you teach your nervous system that laughter, movement,
and delight are safe — even healing.

"When I let joy move through me, life moves with me."

Inner Warmth

The Ritual: Reclaiming the Energy of Play

1. Light the Joy Flame

Light your TrueJoy Joy Candle (grapefruit + lemongrass + vanilla). Watch the flame and smile softly —
yes, smile on purpose.
Whisper: "I invite joy into my space and my spirit." Feel your chest lift slightly as your energy brightens.

*Healing Note: Grapefruit clears emotional heaviness, lemongrass refreshes the mind, and
vanilla opens the heart to pleasure.*

2. Shake Off the Seriousness

Play an upbeat song — something that makes you want to move. Shake your arms, roll your shoulders, sway your hips.
Laugh at how it feels — awkward, funny, alive. Whisper or sing: "I let joy move through me."

*Ancient Wisdom: Indigenous and tribal traditions used dance and laughter as medicine —
movement that shook off grief and called the spirit back into the body.*

3. Anoint with Play Oil

Apply TrueJoy Play Oil (sweet orange + neroli + vanilla) to your wrists and pulse points.
Inhale deeply and repeat: "I give myself permission to play."
Feel your mood lift instantly — this blend opens the sacral chakra, where joy and creative flow reside.

Science Meets Soul: Citrus oils activate dopamine release — the brain's "joy and motivation" messenger.

4. Laughing Breath

Inhale deeply through your nose, then exhale with a soft "haaaaa." Repeat 3–5 times, letting it naturally turn
into a chuckle or smile. If it feels silly, perfect — that's the point. Whisper: "My joy is sacred."

*Healing Note: Laughter increases oxygen, lowers cortisol, and energetically releases heaviness stored
in the diaphragm — the body's emotional center.*

5. Mist for Bliss

Mist TrueJoy Bliss Spray (coconut + lime + jasmine) around your head and shoulders.
Feel it like sunlight on your skin. Whisper: "I radiate joy."

6. Celebrate the Moment

End your ritual by placing your hands over your heart.
Think of one simple thing that brings you joy — a sound, taste, or memory.
Smile again.

Whisper: "Joy lives here."

Journaling

(Use this space to write, draw, or simply breathe into the lessons of today's ritual. There is no right or wrong — only what your soul needs to express.)

Opening the Subconscious Gateway to Wisdom and Guidance

Intention

The night is your soul's quiet classroom.
When you surrender to rest with awareness, your dreams become messengers —
revealing truths, insights, and directions from within.
This ritual bridges waking consciousness and intuitive sleep, helping you
receive guidance with ease.

"I rest with awareness. I awaken with clarity."

Mantra of the Ritual

"In stillness, I see.
In dreams, I remember.
In rest, I awaken."

Optional Enhancements

Keep a dream journal by your bed — write upon waking, even a single
image or feeling. Sleep with amethyst or moonstone nearby to support
intuitive dreaming. Use TrueJoy Moon Oil on temples nightly to signal
the body that it's time to rest and receive.

Healing Integration

Rest is not retreat — it's renewal.
Through sleep, the subconscious integrates your lessons and restores your light.
When you bring intention to your rest, you turn dreaming into an act of awakening.

"The moon teaches that illumination begins in darkness."

Opening the Subconscious Gateway to Wisdom and Guidance

The Ritual: Awakening Through Dreaming

1. Light the Dream Flame

Light your TrueJoy Dream Candle (lavender + sandalwood + mugwort).
Watch the soft glow reflect on your surroundings — allow your breath to slow.
Whisper: "I welcome rest, wisdom, and dreams that guide me."
Healing Note: Mugwort has been used for centuries in Native, Celtic, and Chinese traditions to enhance lucid dreaming and spiritual insight.

2. Anoint the Third Eye & Crown

Rub a few drops of TrueJoy Moon Oil (blue lotus + clary sage + chamomile) between your palms.
Gently press your fingertips to your temples, the space between your brows, and the crown of your head.
Whisper: "I open to the light within the dream."
Ancient Wisdom: Blue lotus was revered in Egyptian rituals as the "flower of consciousness" used to open awareness between worlds.

3. Dream Breath of Release

Sit or lie down comfortably. Inhale through your nose for 4 counts.
Exhale through your mouth for 6, visualizing the day leaving your body as soft light.
Repeat 5–7 rounds, letting your shoulders and jaw relax completely.
With each exhale, silently say: "I release today."
Science Meets Soul: This extended exhale pattern activates the parasympathetic nervous system, signaling safety and preparing the brain for deep rest.

4. Nighttime Reflection

Open your journal and write down one intention for your dreams tonight.
Examples: "Show me what I need to release."
"Help me see my next step clearly."
"Bring healing through rest."
Mist the page lightly with TrueJoy Sleep Mist (lavender + chamomile + neroli).
Close your eyes and visualize moonlight washing over you.
Healing Note: Setting intention before sleep helps the subconscious organize emotional experiences into insight and clarity.

5. Closing the Gateway

Blow out your candle softly.
Whisper: "I surrender to the mystery of rest."
As you lie down, place your right hand on your heart and left hand on your belly.
Feel your breath rise and fall until you drift into sleep.

Journaling

(Use this space to write, draw, or simply breathe into the lessons of today's ritual. There is no right or wrong — only what your soul needs to express.)

Rising into Radiance

Intention

The sun's rising mirrors your own — a daily rebirth.
When you greet the light with presence, you align with life's natural rhythm of awakening. This ritual transforms your morning routine into a ceremony of vitality, gratitude, and self-connection.

"As the sun rises, so do I."

Mantra of the Ritual

"I rise with the sun.
I awaken with grace.
I shine from within."

Optional Enhancements

Step outside barefoot for 1 minute of grounding while facing the sun.
Play gentle instrumental or nature sounds to accompany your ritual.
Follow with light movement — yoga, stretching, or dance —
to circulate morning energy.

Healing Integration

When you greet the light, you greet your soul.
This ritual resets the circadian rhythm, harmonizes your energy field, and grounds you in gratitude. It's not just about waking up — it's about rising aligned.

"The sun does not rush to rise, yet it always arrives on time. So do I."

Aligning with the Day's Energy

The Ritual: Greeting the Light

1. Light the Radiance Flame

Light your TrueJoy Radiance Candle (citrus + ginger + lemongrass).
Watch the flame flicker and brighten, reflecting the first light of day.
Whisper: "I welcome the new light. I am open to renewal."
Inhale the scent deeply — feel it warm your chest, awakening your energy.

Healing Note: Ginger activates circulation, citrus lifts mood, and lemongrass refreshes mental clarity.

2. Awaken the Body

Stand near a window or outdoors where sunlight can reach your face. Take three slow, deep breaths.
Roll your shoulders back, stretch arms overhead, and feel the body lengthen.
Whisper softly: "This is my awakening."

Ancient Wisdom: In Ayurveda, morning movement (Surya Namaskar) honors the body as a vessel for divine light — merging physical and spiritual energy.

3. Anoint with Vitality

Apply TrueJoy Vitality Oil (peppermint + grapefruit + rosemary) to pulse points — wrists, neck, heart.
Inhale the scent and imagine sunlight infusing your cells.
Whisper: "I am alive with purpose."

Science Meets Soul: Rosemary enhances cognitive alertness; peppermint stimulates energy flow and awakens the senses.

4. Drink the Morning Elixir

Mix warm water with a squeeze of lemon and a pinch of turmeric.
Sip slowly as the sun rises.
With each sip, repeat: "I nourish my light."

Healing Note: Lemon detoxifies and alkalizes; turmeric calms inflammation — both awaken internal fire (agni).

5. Set Your Intention

Open your journal and write one word or short phrase that defines how you want to feel today
(e.g., grounded, radiant, open, peaceful).
Mist your space lightly with TrueJoy Clarity Spray (basil + lime + mint).

Whisper: "I move through this day in harmony with my light."

Journaling

(Use this space to write, draw, or simply breathe into the lessons of today's ritual. There is no right or wrong — only what your soul needs to express.)

Translating Desire into Devotion

Intention

Manifestation begins not with asking for more, but with becoming
clear about what truly matters.
When you align intention with emotion, action follows naturally.
This ritual helps you channel your desires into grounded devotion —
calling in what aligns, releasing what distracts.

"I create not by force, but by flow."

Mantra of the Ritual

"I am the bridge between vision and reality.
My clarity creates momentum.
I manifest with ease, not effort."

Optional Enhancements

Perform under the new moon to amplify new beginnings.
Add citrine or clear quartz to your altar to hold frequency of clarity.
Pair with calming music or binaural beats for focus.

Healing Integration

Clarity is the first act of creation — before doing, you become.
This ritual harmonizes the mind's desire with the heart's truth, ensuring what
you call in is not just what you want, but what you're ready to embody.

"Manifestation is not magic — it's alignment made visible."

Translating Desire into Devotion

The Ritual: Anchoring Intention into Form

1. Light the Vision Flame

Light your TrueJoy Vision Candle (sandalwood + orange blossom + cinnamon). Watch the flame and imagine it illuminating your inner world. Whisper: "I awaken clarity within me." Feel warmth expand in your chest, activating your heart's intelligence.

Healing Note: Sandalwood stills the mind, orange blossom lifts creativity, and cinnamon enhances focus and forward motion.

2. Ground Before You Dream

Sit comfortably. Place both feet flat on the ground.
Inhale deeply and exhale through your feet — imagining roots anchoring into the earth.
Whisper: "What I create is rooted in truth." Take three grounding breaths before moving on.

Ancient Wisdom: Manifestation in ancient practice (from Taoist alchemy to Hermetic tradition) began with grounding — connecting heaven's vision to earth's structure.

3. Anoint for Clarity

Apply TrueJoy Manifest Oil (cedarwood + orange + myrrh) to your wrists and temples.
Inhale the scent and visualize a golden spiral of light at your heart expanding outward.
Whisper: "My intention is pure. My vision is clear."

Science Meets Soul: Scent anchors emotion into memory; repeating a phrase while inhaling a scent builds a somatic cue that reinforces focus.

4. Write Your Vision

Open your journal and write freely for 10–15 minutes using these prompts:
What is calling to be created through me right now?
How do I want to feel as I move toward it?
What am I ready to release to make space for it?
Don't censor. Let the writing flow as if your higher self were guiding the pen.

Healing Note: Writing moves intention from thought to form — the first act of materialization.

5. Seal with Sound & Affirmation

Read your intention aloud three times. Mist your space with TrueJoy Abundance Spray
(sweet orange + bergamot + clove). Whisper: "As I speak it, it becomes."
Visualize your words taking root in the earth and expanding into light.

6. Close in Gratitude

Blow out your candle slowly. Place your hand on your heart and say:

"I trust divine timing. I trust my path."

Journaling

(Use this space to write, draw, or simply breathe into the lessons of today's ritual. There is no right or wrong — only what your soul needs to express.)

Transforming Intention into Embodied Movement

Intention

True manifestation requires movement — but not all movement is equal.
When action arises from fear, it drains.
When it flows from inspiration, it expands.
This ritual connects you to your inner guidance, helping you take aligned,
joyful steps toward what you're creating.

"I act with clarity, courage, and trust."

Mantra of the Ritual

"My actions are guided by joy.
My movement is sacred.
My path is unfolding in perfect time."

Optional Enhancements

Play rhythmic instrumental music (drums, strings, or mantra beats) to
fuel movement.
Pair with a sip of warm lemon-ginger tea before taking your action.
Perform this ritual outdoors to harness momentum from nature.

Healing Integration

Action without alignment leads to burnout.
Alignment without action leads to stagnation.
When both merge, momentum becomes magnetic — effortless,
grounded, and guided.
Every small, inspired step affirms to the universe: I am ready.

"When I move with purpose, life moves with me."

Transforming Intention into Embodied Movement
The Ritual: Moving from Intention to Flow
1. Light the Momentum Flame

Light your TrueJoy Momentum Candle (orange + ginger + cardamom). Watch the flame flicker and
grow stronger, mirroring your readiness to move. Whisper: "I am ready to begin."
Inhale deeply and feel your body awaken to possibility.

Healing Note: Orange energizes creativity; ginger ignites willpower; cardamom uplifts emotional courage.

2. Activate the Body

Stand tall with feet hip-width apart. Inhale deeply, raise your arms overhead; exhale, sweep them down.
Repeat three times, letting your breath and body move as one. Whisper: "I align my movement with purpose."

*Ancient Wisdom: In both yogic and Sufi traditions, conscious movement is a form of prayer —
expressing divine energy through embodied rhythm.*

3. Anoint for Motivation

Apply TrueJoy Action Oil (peppermint + clove + bergamot) to wrists and neck.
Inhale deeply, then place your hand over your solar plexus (upper abdomen).
Whisper: "Energy flows where intention goes."

*Science Meets Soul: Peppermint increases alertness, while clove boosts circulation and motivation —
supporting mental focus with physical vitality.*

4. Clarify the Step

Open your journal and write:
What is one inspired action I can take today that moves me closer to my vision?
What is one action I can release that feels forced or draining?
Circle the one that feels lightest — that's your inspired step.
Whisper: "I move in harmony with my truth."

Healing Note: The body often knows what's aligned before the mind does; writing helps the intuition speak clearly.

5. Anchor the Energy

Mist your space with TrueJoy Flow Mist (lemongrass + grapefruit + cedar).
Take one confident step forward and say aloud: "I am in motion. My dreams are alive."
Feel the subtle surge of energy as you shift from intention into movement.

6. Gratitude in Advance

Close your eyes and visualize your action creating ripples of light — reaching others, returning abundance,
expanding joy. Smile and whisper: "I give thanks for what is already unfolding."

Journaling

(Use this space to write, draw, or simply breathe into the lessons of today's ritual. There is no right or wrong — only what your soul needs to express.)

Opening to Flow, Gratitude, and the Energy of Enough

Intention

Abundance is not something you chase — it's something you tune into.
When you embody gratitude and ease, your energy naturally expands to
attract more of what supports your joy.
This ritual helps you shift from efforting to allowing, teaching your nervous
system that it is safe to receive.

"I am open to life's blessings in all forms."

Mantra of the Ritual

"I am open to receiving with ease.
I trust life's flow.
I am abundant, always."

Optional Enhancements

Play soft music with flute, harp, or 528Hz heart frequency.
Pair with a warm cup of cacao or chai to nourish the senses.
Repeat this ritual weekly to rewire your abundance mindset.

Healing Integration

Abundance is not accumulation — it's circulation.
When you receive with gratitude and give with joy, energy flows naturally.
This ritual helps dissolve scarcity patterns by reminding your body that
there is always enough.

"The more I allow, the more I overflow."

Opening to Flow, Gratitude, and the Energy of Enough

The Ritual: Raising the Frequency of Receiving

1. Light the Abundance Flame

Light your TrueJoy Abundance Candle (sweet orange + vanilla + patchouli).
Watch the glow expand as you whisper: "I am surrounded by abundance."
Inhale deeply, allowing your heart to soften and your breath to slow.
Healing Note: Orange uplifts the spirit; vanilla nurtures calm; patchouli grounds abundance into the physical realm.

2. Create a Space of Plenty

Arrange three items that represent abundance for you — a crystal, a flower, a coin, or something from nature.
Place your hands above them, close your eyes, and visualize light radiating from your palms.
Whisper: "What I give, I receive multiplied."
Ancient Wisdom: In ancient Egyptian and Hindu traditions, abundance rituals often involved blessing symbols of prosperity — teaching that gratitude magnetizes flow.

3. Anoint with Worthiness

Apply TrueJoy Receive Oil (geranium + bergamot + sandalwood) over your heart and wrists.
Inhale deeply and whisper: "I am worthy of all that supports my highest good.
Science Meets Soul: Touching the heart while speaking affirmations lowers cortisol and activates the parasympathetic nervous system — opening the body's capacity to receive.

4. Breathe in Expansion

Inhale through your nose for 4 counts, imagining golden light filling your chest.
Hold for 2 counts, feeling the warmth expand.
Exhale slowly through your mouth, releasing resistance.
Repeat for 7 cycles.
Whisper with each inhale: "I receive."
Healing Note: Breath regulates energy flow through the heart and solar plexus — balancing giving and receiving.

5. Gratitude Amplifier

Open your journal and list 10 things you are grateful for — big or small.
After each one, pause and say aloud: "Thank you."
When you finish, close your eyes and feel that gratitude vibrating through your body — warmth, tingling, openness.
Ancient Wisdom: Gratitude is the highest emotional frequency. In nearly every spiritual tradition, it is seen as the seed of abundance.

6. Seal with the Frequency of Flow

Mist your space with TrueJoy Prosperity Spray (cinnamon + orange + frankincense).
Whisper: "Abundance flows to me and through me."
Visualize golden light spiraling through your room, expanding outward infinitely.

Journaling

(Use this space to write, draw, or simply breathe into the lessons of today's ritual. There is no right or wrong — only what your soul needs to express.)

Making the Unseen Seen Through Creative Expression

Intention

Vision is not about seeing the future — it's about feeling it now.
When you visualize your desires with emotion and embodiment, your subconscious begins aligning your choices, energy, and opportunities with that reality.
This ritual transforms your vision from wishful thinking into energetic rehearsal.

"I am already becoming what I envision."

Mantra of the Ritual

"I see it.
I feel it.
I become it."

Daily Practice: 5-Minute Morning Visualization

Each morning, take 5 minutes to sit before your board.
Light a candle.
Breathe deeply.
Choose one image and step into it with your imagination.
Feel gratitude for it as if it already exists.
Whisper: "I am living this with joy."

Healing Integration

Visioning isn't about escaping the present — it's about enriching it with meaning.
When you live today with the emotion of your future, you become a vibrational match for everything you desire.
The universe doesn't respond to words — it responds to frequency.

"My imagination is not fantasy — it is prophecy."

Making the Unseen Seen Through Creative Expression

The Ritual: Giving Form to Your Future

1. Light the Creation Flame

Light your TrueJoy Vision Candle (ylang-ylang + tangerine + sandalwood).
Watch the flame glow and whisper: "I see my dreams clearly."
Inhale deeply, letting your imagination awaken.
Healing Note: Ylang-ylang opens creativity; tangerine inspires optimism; sandalwood grounds the visionary energy into the body.

2. Prepare Your Sacred Space

Gather magazines, printed images, affirmations, or digital tools if you're creating virtually.
Set out your TrueJoy Focus Mist (peppermint + lemon + rosemary).
Mist your area and say: "This space is for creation and clarity."
Ancient Wisdom: Visualization has been used in cultures from Egyptian temple initiations to Tibetan meditation — vision as vibration, not fantasy.

3. Anoint with Creative Flow

Apply TrueJoy Creation Oil (orange blossom + frankincense + jasmine) to your wrists and temples.
Close your eyes for 30 seconds and visualize golden light streaming into your crown and down through your hands.
Whisper: "I channel inspiration with ease."
Science Meets Soul: Engaging the senses during creative focus activates mirror neurons — making visualization feel real, training the nervous system for success.

4. Craft Your Vision Board

Begin placing images or words that evoke the feeling of your desired life — joy, calm, expansion, love, abundance.
Don't overthink. Let intuition guide your hands.
Include symbols of each area of life: Home, career, health, relationships, spirituality, creativity, travel.
Whisper as you work: "I am the artist of my reality."
Healing Note: The act of arranging images translates mental desire into tangible energy, bridging imagination and material creation.

5. Activate the Vision

Sit before your finished board. Lightly place your hands over your heart.
Close your eyes and imagine yourself inside that vision — walking through your dream home,
feeling the sunlight, hearing laughter, experiencing joy.
Whisper: "It is done. I am living this now."
Stay with this feeling for 2–3 minutes.
Ancient Wisdom: Many mystic schools taught "embodied visualization" — the art of living a dream in the present moment to magnetize its arrival.

6. Seal with Faith & Flow

Mist the board with TrueJoy Manifest Mist (geranium + cedarwood + orange).
Whisper: "I trust divine timing and my power to create."
Place the board where you'll see it daily — near your workspace, altar, or mirror.

Journaling

(Use this space to write, draw, or simply breathe into the lessons of today's ritual.
There is no right or wrong — only what your soul needs to express.)

Letting Go with Grace and Staying Rooted in Trust

Intention

Faith is the bridge between intention and manifestation.
It is the quiet knowing that what you desire is already aligning behind the scenes.
This ritual helps you release attachment and anxiety, returning to calm confidence
that everything unfolds in perfect rhythm.

"I release control and trust the flow of life."

Mantra of the Ritual

"I release control with love.
I trust the unfolding.
I am guided, held, and supported."

Optional Enhancements

Pair this ritual with gentle music, sound bowls, or silent meditation.
Perform during the waning moon phase to amplify release energy.
Keep a crystal like rose quartz or moonstone nearby for soft grounding.

Healing Integration

Faith doesn't mean inaction — it means trusting that the energy you've set
in motion is working in your favor.
This ritual rewires the nervous system to find safety in surrender,
helping you rest in divine partnership rather than personal pressure.

"The flower doesn't push to bloom — it opens when it's ready. So do I."

Letting Go with Grace and Staying Rooted in Trust

The Ritual: Letting Go with Grace

1. Light the Trust Flame

Light your TrueJoy Faith Candle (lavender + sandalwood + myrrh).
Watch the flame flicker softly and whisper: "I release all need to control."
Inhale deeply, feeling the tension melt from your shoulders and chest.
Healing Note: Lavender soothes overthinking; sandalwood restores peace; myrrh connects to divine presence.

2. Anoint for Trust

Apply TrueJoy Surrender Oil (rose + frankincense + vetiver) to your pulse points.
Place your right hand over your heart and your left over your abdomen.
Whisper: "I trust the process, even when I can't see it."
*Science Meets Soul: The act of touch calms the vagus nerve — the body's trust signal —
shifting you from control to relaxation.*

3. Release the Tightness

Close your eyes and breathe deeply. As you inhale, imagine soft golden light filling your body.
As you exhale, imagine any tension or fear dissolving like smoke.
Repeat for 7 breaths. Whisper: "I let go with love."
*Ancient Wisdom: In Taoist and yogic traditions, exhalation is sacred — it symbolizes surrender,
the return of control to the divine rhythm of breath.*

4. Fire of Release

Write on a small piece of paper one worry, fear, or attachment that's been weighing on you. Fold it gently.
Hold it near the candle flame (safely) and say aloud: "I release this to the fire of transformation."
Place it in a safe dish to burn or tear it into small pieces, feeling the symbolic release.
Healing Note: Fire alchemizes emotion — it converts resistance into light.

5. The Faith Affirmation

Sit quietly with eyes closed.
Place both hands on your heart and whisper slowly:
"I do not chase what is meant for me.
I rest in divine timing.
I trust that my path is unfolding in grace."
Feel your heartbeat — steady, certain — a physical reminder that life flows effortlessly through you.

6. Seal the Trust

Mist your space with TrueJoy Divine Flow Spray (chamomile + neroli + bergamot).
Whisper: "All is well. All is becoming."
Blow out your candle with intention, visualizing the smoke carrying your surrender to the universe.

Journaling

(Use this space to write, draw, or simply breathe into the lessons of today's ritual. There is no right or wrong — only what your soul needs to express.)

Expanding Your Capacity to Receive from Self-Love, Not Striving

Intention

Manifestation cannot flow through self-doubt.
Your external reality mirrors the way you value yourself internally.
This ritual invites you to release guilt, comparison, and scarcity —
and to open to the truth that you are inherently enough.

"I am worthy of everything aligned with my highest joy."

Mantra of the Ritual

"I am worthy of rest, joy, and abundance.
I receive easily and gratefully.
I am divine by design."

Optional Enhancements

Perform after a bath or self-massage to amplify softness and embodiment.
Pair with rose quartz, rhodonite, or moonstone crystals.
Play soft instrumental or heart chakra frequency (528 Hz) to deepen resonance.

Healing Integration

Self-worth is the soil of manifestation.
Without it, seeds of intention struggle to root.
With it, everything you desire grows effortlessly because it reflects your inner
knowing: I am already enough.
"I no longer chase what I am — I remember it."

Expanding Your Capacity to Receive from Self-Love, Not Striving

The Ritual: Returning to Inherent Worth

1. Light the Self-Love Flame

Light your TrueJoy Worth Candle (rose + vanilla + myrrh).
Gaze softly at the flame, letting its warmth remind you of your own light.
Whisper: "My worth is not earned — it is eternal."
Inhale the scent and exhale tension through the heart center.

Healing Note: Rose opens the heart to love, vanilla nurtures emotional safety, and myrrh grounds you into the sacredness of self.

2. Anoint the Heart with Reverence

Apply TrueJoy Deserve Oil (jasmine + sandalwood + geranium) over your heart and throat.
Close your eyes and rest your hand there. Whisper: "It is safe to receive."
Feel the heartbeat — steady and deserving — as a reminder of your constant enoughness.

Ancient Wisdom: In Egyptian and Vedic tradition, the heart was seen as the seat of truth — worth measured not by doing, but by being in harmony with one's essence.

3. Mirror Reflection Ceremony

Stand before a mirror.
Look directly into your own eyes and say: "I see you. You are worthy of love, joy, abundance, and rest."
Repeat three times, letting emotion rise if it needs to.
Afterward, place both hands on your heart and take three deep breaths of gratitude.

Science Meets Soul: Mirror work activates self-recognition in the brain, reducing shame and increasing self-compassion over time.

4. Journal of Deserving

In your journal, answer these prompts slowly:
Where in my life do I still feel I must earn my worth?
Who taught me to doubt my value — and can I forgive them?
What does receiving with ease feel like in my body?
What would I allow if I fully believed I was worthy?
After writing, whisper: "I release the old story. I choose truth."

Healing Note: Writing transforms subconscious beliefs into conscious awareness — the first step in rewriting them.

5. Affirm and Anchor

Mist your space with TrueJoy Self-Love Mist (rose + neroli + chamomile).
Close your eyes and visualize a radiant pink light filling your aura, pulsing gently like a heartbeat.
Whisper: "My worth is unwavering. I receive with grace."

6. Seal with Gratitude

Blow out your candle and place your hand over your heart once more.
Whisper: "I honor the one who has always been enough."

Journaling

(Use this space to write, draw, or simply breathe into the lessons of today's ritual.
There is no right or wrong — only what your soul needs to express.)

Creating Momentum with Grace and Trust

Intention

Action born from flow feels like peace in motion.
It's not about forcing results — it's about moving from inner guidance and energetic alignment. This ritual reconnects you to inspired productivity — where focus meets intuition, and effort becomes devotion.

"I create with rhythm, not rush."

Mantra of the Ritual

"I work from inspiration, not obligation.
I act with clarity, move with grace, and rest in flow."

Optional Enhancements

Play lo-fi, ambient, or binaural focus music during work sessions.
Keep a carnelian or citrine crystal on your desk for motivation and energy.
Use this ritual before creative projects, writing, or important calls.

Healing Integration

Balance is creation in harmony.
This ritual reminds you that productivity isn't about doing more —
it's about doing with meaning.
When action and intuition merge, your output multiplies while your stress dissolves.

"When I move with the current, everything I need arrives effortlessly."

Creating Momentum with Grace and Trust

The Ritual: Merging Momentum and Mindfulness

1. Light the Flow Flame

Light your TrueJoy Flow Candle (grapefruit + cedarwood + basil).vWatch the flame flicker with steady grace —
neither hurried nor still. Whisper: "I move in rhythm with life."
Inhale deeply and imagine the scent energizing your solar plexus.
*Healing Note: Grapefruit uplifts, cedarwood grounds, basil clarifies —
the perfect trio for balanced, focused flow.*

2. Anoint for Balance

Apply TrueJoy Harmony Oil (mint + lemongrass + frankincense) to wrists and temples.
As you inhale, imagine energy flowing smoothly through your entire body.
Whisper: "I act from peace, not pressure."
*Ancient Wisdom: In Eastern philosophy, balance of masculine (yang) and feminine (yin) energy sustains
creativity and life force — discipline guided by flow.*

3. The Rhythm Breath

Sit or stand tall. Inhale for 4 counts (inspiration). Hold for 2 (integration).
Exhale for 6 (release). Continue for 2–3 minutes, visualizing your breath as a wave moving in and out.
Whisper: "I am the tide — steady and strong."
*Science Meets Soul: This breath pattern balances the sympathetic and parasympathetic systems —
sharpening focus while calming stress.*

4. Intuitive Planning

Open your journal and divide a page into two columns:
Effort: "What requires my action today?"
Ease: "Where can I allow flow to guide me?"
Fill in both sides intuitively, without judgment.
Whisper: "I balance effort with trust."
*Healing Note: Writing from both hemispheres of the brain (logical and intuitive) creates integrated
focus — the essence of flow state creation.*

5. Mini Movement Reset

Stand up and gently shake out the body for 30 seconds.
Roll your shoulders, sway your hips, and reconnect to breath.
Feel energy shifting from mental effort to embodied rhythm.
Whisper: "Work becomes sacred when I move with it."

6. Seal with Surrender

Mist your space with TrueJoy Focus & Flow Spray (peppermint + lavender + lime).
Whisper: "I am both the wave and the stillness beneath it."
Sit for one minute in silence, letting this energy integrate.

Journaling

(Use this space to write, draw, or simply breathe into the lessons of today's ritual.
There is no right or wrong — only what your soul needs to express.)

Clearing the Old, Inviting the New

Intention

Renewal begins when you stop trying to go back.
Every breath, every sunrise, every season whispers: "You are allowed to start again."
This ritual helps your body, heart, and energy field let go of what's complete — and open fully to the beauty of the unknown.
"I welcome new beginnings with peace and grace."

Mantra of the Ritual

"I release what was.
I open to what is.
I am renewed, reborn, and free."

Optional Enhancements

Perform this ritual at sunrise for extra renewal energy.
Place a fresh flower or crystal (clear quartz, green aventurine) on your altar.
End with a cup of herbal tea — mint or chamomile — to ground your new energy.

Healing Integration

Renewal is not rushing toward the next goal — it's resting in readiness.
When you surrender to cycles, life renews you naturally.
This ritual restores energetic flow, emotional lightness, and faith in what's unfolding.

"Nothing is lost — everything is transforming."

Clearing the Old, Inviting the New

The Ritual: Clearing and Calling In Renewal

1. Light the Renewal Flame

Light your TrueJoy Renewal Candle (lemon + eucalyptus + sage). Watch the flame flicker
clean and bright, symbolizing clarity. Whisper: "As this flame burns, I release what is no longer
mine to carry." Take three deep breaths — each exhale washing away the old.
*Healing Note: Lemon clears stagnant energy, eucalyptus opens the breath and lungs, and sage purifies
the aura — awakening clarity and courage for what's next.*

2. Anoint with Rebirth

Apply TrueJoy Rebirth Oil (lavender + neroli + rosemary) to your temples, wrists, and heart.
As you inhale, visualize your energy field refreshing — like sunlight filtering through clean water.
Whisper: "I am renewed from within."
*Ancient Wisdom: In ancient Egyptian and Roman cultures, fragrant oils were used for purification during
seasonal transitions — believed to cleanse emotional residue and renew vitality.*

3. Water of Letting Go

Fill a bowl with warm water (or take this ritual into your bath or shower).
Add a pinch of sea salt and a few drops of TrueJoy Rebirth Oil or fresh herbs (mint, rosemary, or basil).
Swirl the water clockwise, whispering: "I release the past. I welcome the flow of new beginnings."
Dip your hands into the water and pour it over your heart or crown.
Imagine the water washing away old emotions, expectations, and attachments.
*Science Meets Soul: Water soothes the vagus nerve — the body's "calm signal" — grounding the nervous
system and inviting a sense of renewal.*

4. Breath of Beginning

Sit comfortably with both feet on the ground.
Inhale through your nose for 4 counts (receive), hold for 2 (integrate), and exhale for 6 (release).
With each breath, whisper inwardly:
"Inhale: I receive renewal.
Exhale: I release the past."
Continue for 7 rounds, feeling your heart soften and your energy lighten.
Healing Note: The breath resets emotional rhythm — signaling to your body that it's safe to move forward.

5. Journal of Renewal

What season of my life is naturally ending?
What energy or pattern am I ready to release?
What qualities do I want to embody in this new chapter?
How can I move forward with softness, not urgency?
Write freely. Then close your journal and whisper: "I honor what was. I bless what is becoming."

6. Seal the Energy

Mist your space with TrueJoy Renewal Mist (lemongrass + peppermint + white tea).
Whisper: "I am light. I am new. I am ready."
Visualize your aura expanding with golden-green light — the frequency of fresh beginnings.

Journaling

(Use this space to write, draw, or simply breathe into the lessons of today's ritual. There is no right or wrong — only what your soul needs to express.)

Transforming Judgment into Understanding and Wholeness

Intention

Your shadow is not your enemy — it's the unseen part of your light.
This ritual invites you to meet yourself beyond shame or judgment, turning hidden aspects into wisdom and power.
When you embrace your shadow, you evolve from fragmentation to wholeness.

"I am the light and the shadow — both make me whole."

Mantra of the Ritual

"I am whole, worthy, and complete.
My light needs my shadow to shine.
I honor all that I am."

Optional Enhancements

Perform this ritual on a dark or rainy evening to embrace nature's mirror.
Use a black tourmaline or obsidian crystal for grounding.
End with a gentle self-hug — symbolizing reunion with self.

Healing Integration

Shadow work is soul retrieval.
It brings lost power, creativity, and truth back home to your heart.
When you stop rejecting parts of yourself, you stop rejecting life itself.

"My shadow does not make me broken — it makes me real."

Transforming Judgment into Understanding and Wholeness
The Ritual: Illuminating the Hidden Within
1. Light the Illumination Flame

Light your TrueJoy Shadow Candle (patchouli + amber + clove).
Watch how the shadows dance on the wall — reminders that darkness only exists where light shines.
Whisper: "I welcome all parts of me into the light of awareness."
Inhale deeply, grounding yourself in presence.

Healing Note: Patchouli roots the spirit, amber balances emotion, and clove activates courage and strength.

2. Anoint with Acceptance

Apply TrueJoy Wholeness Oil (vetiver + rose + cedarwood) to your wrists and solar plexus.
Close your eyes and whisper: "I honor every version of me — the seen and unseen."
Feel warmth building where judgment used to live.

Ancient Wisdom: In Jungian and tantric teachings, integration of shadow restores balance — uniting the conscious and unconscious as divine wholeness.

3. Mirror of Truth

Sit before a mirror in soft light (candlelight is ideal).
Look into your eyes and simply observe — no correction, no story.
Whisper softly: "I see you. I accept you. I forgive you. I love you."
Let emotion arise — tears, laughter, or stillness — and breathe through it.

Science Meets Soul: Mirror work increases self-compassion and activates self-awareness networks in the brain, creating neural pathways for acceptance.

4. Shadow Journal Inquiry

Open your TrueJoy Evolve Journal and write:
What qualities in others trigger me — and what part of me do they mirror?
What emotions or behaviors do I hide from others?
What truth have I been afraid to admit about myself?
How can I bring love to that part of me today?
After writing, close your journal gently and whisper: "I am no longer divided. I am whole."
Healing Note: Writing shadow truths moves them from the subconscious into the light of conscious healing.

5. Candle of Integration

Take a few deep breaths and gaze again at the candle flame.
Imagine light slowly expanding from your heart to embrace every part of your being — your strength, fears, regrets, and gifts. Whisper: "All that I am is sacred."
Feel peace spreading through your body like a warm glow.

6. Seal with Compassion

Mist your space with TrueJoy Integration Mist (lavender + black pepper + sandalwood).
Whisper: "I welcome every part of me into love."
Sit quietly for one minute, feeling balance, stillness, and acceptance.

Journaling

(Use this space to write, draw, or simply breathe into the lessons of today's ritual. There is no right or wrong — only what your soul needs to express.)

Transforming Emotion into Light and Power

Intention

Emotions are energy — they are not meant to be suppressed, but transmuted. When you sit with them consciously, they become teachers, not tormentors. This ritual helps you move through emotional density with awareness and love until it transforms into wisdom.

"What once hurt me now heals me."

Mantra of the Ritual

"I honor my feelings as sacred teachers.
I transform pain into purpose, grief into grace.
I am the alchemist of my soul."

Optional Enhancements

Perform under the full moon for amplified release and renewal.
Use smoky quartz or carnelian crystals for emotional grounding and transformation.
Play 396Hz or 528Hz frequencies to support emotional repair.

Healing Integration

True evolution happens when you stop running from emotion and start learning from it.
This ritual reminds you that nothing within you is wasted — every experience can become light if met with love.

"My emotions are not my weakness — they are my transformation."

Transforming Emotion into Light and Power
The Ritual: Alchemizing Emotion into Light

1. Light the Alchemy Flame

Light your TrueJoy Transmutation Candle (amber + rose + vetiver).
Watch the flame — its soft flicker symbolizes emotion turning into illumination.
Whisper: "From this flame, I awaken the light within my pain."

Healing Note: Amber carries ancestral strength, rose opens the heart, and vetiver grounds the emotional body for safe release.

2. Anoint for Courage

Apply TrueJoy Alchemy Oil (frankincense + clary sage + geranium) to your chest and solar plexus.
As you inhale, feel calm courage expanding inside you.
Whisper: "It is safe to feel. It is safe to heal."

Ancient Wisdom: Alchemists believed transformation began not in gold, but in the heart — where dense emotion became clarity through awareness.

3. Breath of Transformation

Inhale deeply through your nose for 4 counts, feeling the emotion rise. Hold for 2 counts — acknowledge it fully. Exhale through your mouth for 6 counts — release resistance.
Repeat 7 cycles. Whisper: "With each breath, I transform emotion into wisdom."

Science Meets Soul: Conscious breathing oxygenates the brain and lowers cortisol, making the body feel safe enough to process deep emotion.

4. Dialogue with the Emotion

Sit with your journal and write: "Dear emotion, what are you trying to teach me?"
"Where in my life have I felt this before?" "What new wisdom are you revealing?"
Let the emotion speak — without judgment, without censorship.
Then respond: "Thank you for showing me what I needed to see."

Healing Note: Naming emotion integrates it — the brain moves it from the emotional limbic system into higher reasoning centers.

5. Fire of Transmutation

Write one word that captures what you are ready to transform (e.g., fear, guilt, anger).
Safely hold it near your Transmutation Candle flame and let it burn in a fire-safe dish.
Whisper: "This emotion now becomes light."
Visualize the smoke rising as energy returning purified to the universe.

Ancient Wisdom: Fire ceremonies were used in nearly every culture — from the Vedic homa to Celtic Beltane — to symbolize the transformation of density into clarity.

6. Seal with Stillness

Mist your space with TrueJoy Phoenix Spray (citrus + myrrh + patchouli).
Whisper: "From my pain, beauty is born."
Sit in silence for one minute, letting peace replace intensity.

Journaling

(Use this space to write, draw, or simply breathe into the lessons of today's ritual. There is no right or wrong — only what your soul needs to express.)

Becoming the Safe Space You Always Needed

Intention

You cannot evolve through pressure — only through permission.
This ritual helps you release self-criticism, practice emotional gentleness,
and cultivate loving awareness toward every part of yourself.

"I meet myself with tenderness."

Mantra of the Ritual

"I am gentle with myself.
I evolve through love, not pressure.
My softness is my strength."

Optional Enhancements

Perform in candlelight or after a warm bath for deeper relaxation.
Wrap yourself in a blanket — symbolic of self-embrace.
End with herbal tea (chamomile, rose, or lavender).

Healing Integration

Self-compassion is what turns survival into healing.
It teaches you that the way you speak to yourself is your frequency — and that
love, spoken inward, changes everything.

"When I am kind to myself, everything heals faster."

Becoming the Safe Space You Always Needed
The Ritual: Loving Yourself Back Into Wholeness

1. Light the Compassion Flame

Light your TrueJoy Self-Love Candle (vanilla + rose + chamomile).
As it flickers, place your hand over your heart and whisper: "I am safe to love myself completely."
Breathe deeply, letting the aroma remind your nervous system that it's safe to soften.
Healing Note: Rose heals emotional wounds, chamomile calms anxiety, and vanilla releases the body's oxytocin response — increasing warmth and peace.

2. Anoint with Kindness

Apply TrueJoy Nurture Oil (lavender + sweet orange + ylang-ylang) to your chest, neck, and shoulders.
As you massage it in, say aloud: "I forgive myself for forgetting my softness."
Imagine warmth melting any tension or self-blame.
Ancient Wisdom: In Ayurvedic and Egyptian traditions, oiling the body (abhyanga) was considered an act of love — a reminder that touch is nourishment for the soul.

3. Heart Breath of Compassion

Inhale deeply into your heart for 4 counts, imagining soft pink light expanding. Hold for 2 counts —
let it fill your chest. Exhale slowly for 6 counts, releasing judgment and tension.
Whisper: "I am enough. I am safe. I am loved."
Repeat for 7 breaths.
Science Meets Soul: Compassion-focused breathing increases serotonin and activates the parasympathetic nervous system — the body's "rest and restore" state.

4. Mirror of Grace

Sit before a mirror or hold a photo of yourself.
Look into your eyes and gently say: "You've done your best. I'm proud of you. I love you."
Let emotion rise naturally — tears, smiles, or quiet stillness are all sacred.
Allow this to be your personal moment of reunion.
Healing Note: Eye-gazing with oneself builds self-trust and rewires inner dialogue — replacing criticism with compassion.

5. Letter of Loving Acknowledgment

In your TrueJoy Evolve Journal, write a short note beginning with:
"Dear Me, thank you for..."
List everything you appreciate about yourself — the strength, the softness, the survival.
Then write:
"I release the need to be perfect. I choose to be present."
Close the journal with your hand on your heart and whisper: "I am love embodied."

6. Seal with Peace

Mist your space with TrueJoy Heart Mist (rosewater + jasmine + bergamot).
Whisper: "May I always meet myself with kindness."
Sit in stillness, feeling your body soften and your breath steady.

Journaling

(Use this space to write, draw, or simply breathe into the lessons of today's ritual. There is no right or wrong — only what your soul needs to express.)

Aligning with Nature's Rhythm and Your Own Inner Seasons

Intention

There is no rush in nature — and yet, everything blooms in time.
This ritual helps you honor the natural rhythm of your healing and growth,
teaching you to listen to the wisdom of your inner seasons instead of
forcing constant productivity.

"I honor my seasons — each one brings its own beauty."

Mantra of the Ritual

"I honor the rhythm of my life.
I bloom, rest, release, and rise — all in divine time."

Optional Enhancements

Track your emotional and energy cycles with the moon or seasons.
Create a small altar with one item from each season (flower, leaf, stone, candle).
End with herbal tea — ginger in winter, mint in summer.

Healing Integration

You are not meant to be endless summer.
The stillness of winter, the letting go of autumn, and the rebirth of spring
are all sacred parts of becoming.
This ritual teaches harmony with life's rhythm — and peace in the pause.

"Nothing blooms all year — and that's the beauty of it."

Aligning with Nature's Rhythm and Your Own Inner Seasons

The Ritual: Moving in Harmony with Life's Rhythm

1. Light the Rhythm Flame

Light your TrueJoy Cycles Candle (cedarwood + orange + clove).
Watch how the flame wavers, then steadies — just like your own journey.
Whisper: "I move with the rhythm of my life."
Healing Note: Cedarwood grounds, orange uplifts, and clove ignites vitality — a symbolic trio of grounding, joy, and warmth through all seasons.

2. Anoint with Earth's Rhythm

Apply TrueJoy Flow of Seasons Oil (geranium + patchouli + grapefruit) to your wrists and lower belly.
Whisper: "I trust the timing of my growth."
Feel the scent anchor you into the cyclical nature of your body and energy.
Ancient Wisdom: Indigenous and Ayurvedic traditions both tracked personal energy by the moon and seasons — aligning self-care, rest, and creation with nature's timing to restore balance.

3. Elemental Reflection

In your Journal, draw four circles representing the seasons. Reflect on each:
Spring — Renewal: What's beginning?
Summer — Expansion: Where am I thriving?
Autumn — Release: What am I shedding?
Winter — Stillness: Where am I called to rest?
Write freely under each, allowing clarity to rise. Whisper: "Each season has a lesson — I receive them all."
Science Meets Soul: Research on seasonal affect and circadian rhythms shows our hormones, mood, and creativity ebb and flow naturally — syncing with the Earth's rotation and light cycles.

4. Movement of Seasons

Stand with feet grounded, arms loose. Flow gently through four motions representing each season:
Spring: arms opening wide — welcoming.
Summer: reach high — receiving light.
Autumn: slow bow forward — releasing.
Winter: arms crossed over chest — resting. Repeat the cycle three times, breathing deeply.
Whisper: "I move as nature moves — in flow, not force."
Healing Note: Movement creates rhythm awareness — reconnecting body and emotion with nature's cycles.

5. Moonlight Gratitude

If possible, perform this under moonlight (or near a window).
Whisper: "Just as the moon changes, so do I — and both are beautiful."
Place your Cycles Candle nearby and breathe in its glow.

6. Seal the Ritual

Mist your space with TrueJoy Seasons Mist (sage + lemongrass + lavender).
Whisper: "I am in rhythm with life."
Sit in quiet reflection, feeling harmony between your breath, your body, and the Earth's pulse.

Journaling

(Use this space to write, draw, or simply breathe into the lessons of today's ritual. There is no right or wrong — only what your soul needs to express.)

Turning Every Experience Into Wisdom and Light

Intention

Every experience carries a message.
When you approach your past with gratitude instead of resentment, you reclaim
your energy from it — and your story becomes your strength.
"I am grateful for the wisdom my journey has given me."

Mantra of the Ritual

"I thank the past for its wisdom.
I release pain, keep the lesson, and rise with grace."

Optional Enhancements

Perform this ritual with soft golden light or sunset glow.
Write a letter of gratitude to your younger self.
End with a cup of golden milk or herbal tea as a self-honoring gesture.

Healing Integration

Gratitude is the alchemist of emotion — it turns memory into meaning and
pain into peace. You evolve when you can look at the past and say,
"It didn't break me — it built me."

"I walk forward in gratitude, not grief."

Turning Every Experience Into Wisdom and Light
The Ritual: Transforming Reflection into Empowerment
1. Light the Gratitude Flame
Light your TrueJoy Gratitude Candle (citrus + vanilla + sandalwood).
Gaze softly at the flame and whisper: "I bless my past and thank it for the lessons it brought."
As you breathe, imagine the glow warming your chest — melting any leftover resistance or regret.
Healing Note: Citrus uplifts mood, vanilla soothes the nervous system, and sandalwood connects the mind to higher perspective.

2. Anoint for Wisdom
Apply TrueJoy Empowerment Oil (frankincense + orange blossom + cedar).
Place your hand on your heart and whisper: "Every challenge refined me. Every lesson strengthened me."
Feel your energy stabilize — a merging of past, present, and purpose.
Ancient Wisdom: In Tibetan and Stoic philosophy, gratitude was seen as the bridge between suffering and enlightenment — a recognition that everything serves the soul's evolution.

3. Journal of Lessons
In your Journal, write three columns: Reflect on:
A time you faced fear but acted anyway.
A relationship that taught you self-worth.
A loss that deepened your compassion.
Afterward, write a closing statement: "I honor all that has shaped me — I am the wisdom of my journey."
Science Meets Soul: Writing reflections of gratitude rewires the brain — increasing optimism, lowering stress, and reinforcing emotional resilience.

4. Symbolic Offering
Hold a small stone, leaf, or flower in your hand. Whisper: "I release the weight. I keep the wisdom.
" Place it in nature, or keep it on your altar as a reminder that you grow through everything.
Healing Note: Physical offering symbolizes energetic completion — giving back to the Earth what you no longer need.

5. Gratitude Breath
Inhale slowly through your nose for 4 counts — receive gratitude.
Hold for 2 counts — integrate the lesson.
Exhale gently for 6 counts — release the pain.
Repeat 7 times, letting your breath feel like forgiveness and appreciation interwoven.

6. Seal the Ritual
Mist your space with TrueJoy Reflection Spray (rose + neroli + bergamot).
Whisper: "I am at peace with my story."
Sit in stillness, feeling warmth in your chest — the energetic frequency of gratitude.

Journaling

(Use this space to write, draw, or simply breathe into the lessons of today's ritual. There is no right or wrong — only what your soul needs to express.)

Exhale the Old, Inhale the New

Intention

The breath is the quiet teacher of transformation.
It reminds you that change is not something you chase — it's something you
allow, one inhale and exhale at a time.

"With every breath, I become more of who I am."

Mantra of the Ritual

"I breathe in possibility.
I exhale the past.
With every breath, I become."

Optional Enhancements

Perform at sunrise for new beginnings or at dusk for emotional release.
Use soft flute or ocean wave sound to deepen rhythm.
Add gentle movement like shoulder rolls or stretches between breath cycles.

Healing Integration

Breath bridges the physical and spiritual — the body's reminder that presence is power.
Through conscious breathing, you move beyond thought and back into truth:
that you are always evolving, one inhale at a time.

"Transformation is not effort — it's breath."

Exhale the Old, Inhale the New
The Ritual: Awakening Through Breath
1. Light the Breath Candle

Light your TrueJoy Awakening Candle (peppermint + eucalyptus + cedar).
Watch how the flame moves with your breath — alive, fluid, responsive.
Whisper: "As I breathe, I awaken the new within me."
Healing Note: Peppermint opens the lungs and clarity centers, eucalyptus expands breath flow, and cedar grounds the body's energy.

2. Anoint for Flow

Apply TrueJoy Breath Oil (lavender + lemon + frankincense) to your temples, chest, and under the nose.
Inhale deeply, noticing the cooling and calming blend.
Whisper: "Each breath purifies, balances, and renews me."
Ancient Wisdom: In yogic tradition, prana (life force) is carried on the breath — seen as divine energy that renews and sustains life itself.

3. The Breath of Becoming Practice

Find a comfortable seat or lie down. Rest one hand on your heart, one on your belly.
Begin this 3-part breath pattern: Cycle (5 minutes):
Inhale through your nose for 4 counts — receive.
Hold gently for 2 counts — absorb.
Exhale through your mouth for 6 counts — release.
Cycle (5 minutes): Inhale: "I welcome change."
Exhale: "I release fear."
Cycle (5 minutes):
Inhale: "I am becoming."
Exhale: "I am free."
Science Meets Soul: Slow rhythmic breathing balances the vagus nerve, lowers cortisol, and shifts brainwaves into alpha — the state of calm awareness where transformation naturally unfolds.

4. Energy Flow Visualization

As you breathe, imagine golden light entering through your inhale.
See it move through your body, gathering stagnation or heaviness.
On your exhale, visualize that energy leaving as mist — dissolving back into light.
Whisper: "With each breath, I am renewed."
Healing Note: Visualization engages the body's biofeedback — aligning intention and physiology for deeper calm.

5. Journal of Becoming

In your Journal, write: What am I ready to breathe life into?
Who am I becoming when I release resistance?
How can my daily breath remind me that transformation is gentle?
Close the page with your hands over your heart and whisper: "I am alive with new energy."

6. Seal with Stillness

Mist your space with TrueJoy Renewal Spray (lemongrass + neroli + mint).
Sit in silence for one minute, simply breathing and being.
Whisper: "My breath carries me home."

Journaling

(Use this space to write, draw, or simply breathe into the lessons of today's ritual. There is no right or wrong — only what your soul needs to express.)

Reclaiming Courage, Trust, and Forward Momentum

Intention

Fear is not the enemy — it's the messenger that points toward growth.
When you meet fear with presence and love, it transforms into clarity and courage.
This ritual helps you turn the energy of fear into your greatest ally for empowerment.

"I do not fight fear — I free it."

Mantra of the Ritual

"I breathe through fear into freedom.
My courage is my calm.
I am powerful, present, and free."

Optional Enhancements

Play empowering instrumental or drum-based music
(rhythmic tempo around 80–100 bpm).
Hold tiger's eye or red jasper crystals for grounding courage.
Perform at sunrise to symbolize awakening bravery.

Healing Integration

Fear loses power when met with love and attention.
This ritual retrains the nervous system to respond to challenge with calm focus — teaching that bravery is not the absence of fear, but the ability to move with it gracefully.

"I no longer run from fear — I rise with it."

Reclaiming Courage, Trust, and Forward Momentum
The Ritual: Transforming Fear into Power
1. Light the Courage Flame

Light your TrueJoy Power Candle (black pepper + cedar + orange).
Watch the flame steady itself and whisper: "As this flame rises, so does my courage."
Feel your feet on the ground — rooted, strong, supported.

Healing Note: Black pepper ignites willpower, cedar grounds energy, and orange opens creative action and positivity.

2. Anoint for Strength

Apply TrueJoy Courage Oil (rosemary + frankincense + ginger) to your chest, wrists, and temples.
Whisper: "I transform fear into focus. I am safe to move forward."
Feel your chest expand — the body's way of saying, I'm ready.

Ancient Wisdom: In Roman tradition, warriors anointed themselves with spiced oils before battle to awaken alertness and calm the nerves — honoring courage through ritual, not force.

3. Grounding Breath for Safety

Inhale through your nose for 4 counts, feel your belly rise.
Hold for 2 counts — whisper: "I am safe."
Exhale through your mouth for 6 counts, releasing tension.
Repeat for 7 breaths, anchoring into calm strength.

Science Meets Soul: Grounded breathing regulates the vagus nerve, signaling the body that fear can be processed without reactivity — transforming it into awareness and focus.

4. Journal of Fear to Freedom

In your Journal, write:
What fear am I currently facing?
What truth is this fear trying to reveal to me?
What action or boundary will move me closer to freedom?
Then, in bold letters, write: "I choose courage over comfort."
Healing Note: Naming fear gives it shape — and once it's seen, it loses control.

5. Fire of Fear Release

Write one sentence on a small piece of paper beginning with "I release the fear of..."
Safely hold it near your Power Candle flame and let it burn in a dish.
Whisper: "Fear, I thank you for protecting me. I now release you to light."
Watch the smoke rise — the energy of fear dissolving into strength.

6. Seal the Energy

Mist your aura with TrueJoy Power Mist (bergamot + lemon + sage).
Stand tall and whisper: "I walk in courage. I stand in power. I act from truth."
Breathe deeply and feel energy moving upward through your spine — alive and ready.

Journaling

(Use this space to write, draw, or simply breathe into the lessons of today's ritual.
There is no right or wrong — only what your soul needs to express.)

Standing Tall, Grounded, and Unshakably Aligned

Intention

Your posture tells the world what you believe about yourself —
but more importantly, it tells your nervous system.
When you embody confidence physically, your energy follows.
This ritual helps you retrain your body to stand, breathe, and move from power —
not tension.

"I don't wait to feel confident. I embody confidence now."

Mantra of the Ritual

"My body remembers strength.
My breath restores calm.
My energy radiates confidence."

Optional Enhancements

Play empowering instrumental music (deep drums or cinematic tones).
Practice "mountain pose" or "warrior II" from yoga to embody presence.
Repeat this ritual for 7 mornings to build a confidence rhythm.

Healing Integration

Confidence is not built — it's remembered.
When your body feels safe and aligned, your energy naturally expands into
its full potential.
This ritual turns posture into prayer —
a living expression of your inner strength.

"Power is not loud — it's grounded."

Standing Tall, Grounded, and Unshakably Aligned
The Ritual: Grounding Power Through Posture
1. Light the Confidence Flame

Light your TrueJoy Empower Candle (lemon + cedar + rosemary). Stand tall as it flickers and whisper: "As this flame rises, so do I." Feel your feet plant into the Earth — strong, steady, unmovable.
Healing Note: Lemon uplifts the mind, cedar stabilizes energy, and rosemary enhances clarity and focus — a trio for empowerment.

2. Anoint for Strength

Apply TrueJoy Empower Oil (black pepper + cypress + vanilla) to your wrists and along your spine.
Whisper: "I embody my power with grace."
Inhale deeply and exhale through the mouth — a physical release of doubt.
Ancient Wisdom: In martial traditions and yoga lineages alike, breath and posture were considered tools to command energy — prana — and direct intention into action.

3. The 5-Step Power Alignment Practice

Step 1: Ground
Stand barefoot, feet hip-width apart. Press evenly through all four corners of your feet. Whisper: "I am supported."
Step 2: Breathe
Inhale through your nose for 4 counts, expanding your chest. Exhale slowly for 6 counts, relaxing shoulders.
Whisper: "I am calm."
Step 3: Align
Roll shoulders back and down. Lift chin slightly and soften your jaw. Engage your core gently. Whisper: "I am steady."
Step 4: Expand
Stretch your arms wide, palms forward. Feel energy radiating from your heart space outward.
Whisper: "I am powerful."
Step 5: Anchor
Place hands on your heart. Close your eyes and smile softly. Whisper: "I am confident in who I am."
Science Meets Soul: Standing in a power posture for even 2 minutes increases testosterone (confidence hormone) and reduces cortisol (stress hormone), reinforcing an inner state of calm authority.

4. Mirror Affirmation

Stand before a mirror, look into your own eyes, and say: "I trust myself. I stand in my truth."
I am the energy I want to attract."
Repeat three times — slow, intentional, grounded.
Healing Note: The nervous system begins to associate upright posture and strong breath with safety, creating a new embodied memory of strength.

5. Journal of Empowered Presence

In your Journal, write: What does confidence feel like in my body?
Where do I collapse my energy or shrink? How can I remind myself daily to stand in power?
End with a declaration: "I embody confidence, clarity, and calm strength."

6. Seal the Energy

Mist your aura with TrueJoy Empower Mist (orange + mint + sandalwood).
Whisper: "I walk with grounded confidence and radiant peace."
Visualize yourself walking through the day as light — steady, composed, magnetic.

Journaling

(Use this space to write, draw, or simply breathe into the lessons of today's ritual.
There is no right or wrong — only what your soul needs to express.)

Saying No from Love, Power, and Truth

Intention

"No" is not rejection — it's redirection.
It's how your soul protects your energy and aligns you with what truly matters.
This ritual teaches you to see "No" as sacred — an act of love for yourself and others.

"My No is sacred. My No is love."

Mantra of the Ritual

"My No is sacred.
My No is peace.
I honor myself and trust that love remains."

Optional Enhancements

Use a rose quartz or turquoise crystal to amplify throat chakra balance.
Play low drum or cello music to stabilize energy before speaking your truth.
Perform this ritual before writing or sending a boundary-setting message.

Healing Integration

Every "No" creates space for your "Yes" to flourish.
When you say no with peace and love, you stop betraying your energy —
and life begins to trust your alignment again.

"When I stop overgiving, I start overflowing."

Saying No from Love, Power, and Truth
The Ritual: Reclaiming the Sacred Power of No
1. Light the Empowerment Flame

Light your TrueJoy Truth Candle (amber + myrrh + black pepper).
Whisper: "As this flame burns, I speak truth without fear."
Watch it glow and breathe deeply into your chest — where courage lives.
Healing Note: Amber restores courage, myrrh clears self-doubt, and black pepper ignites assertiveness.

2. Anoint for Clarity

Apply TrueJoy Clarity Oil (eucalyptus + lemon + frankincense) to your temples, throat, and wrists.
Whisper: "My words are clear. My heart is kind. My No is sacred."
Feel energy gathering in your throat — the voice center — ready to express truth calmly and confidently.
Ancient Wisdom: In Egyptian temples, frankincense was burned to purify communication and bring words into alignment with divine integrity.

3. Ground in Self-Trust

Place both hands on your heart.
Take 5 slow breaths — inhale through the nose, exhale through the mouth.
Whisper: "I trust myself to know what feels right."
Feel warmth spreading through your chest as you reconnect to your intuitive yes and no.
Science Meets Soul: Deep diaphragmatic breathing rebalances the heart-brain connection — strengthening self-trust and emotional regulation before communication.

4. The Sacred No Practice

Take out your Journal and write:
What situations drain my energy or compromise my peace?
Where do I say yes when I mean no — and why?
What does a "Sacred No" look and feel like in my body?
Read them aloud slowly, as if making an oath to yourself.
Healing Note: Saying "No" from love teaches the body that safety and sovereignty coexist — building emotional security and self-respect.

5. Voice Activation

Stand or sit tall, shoulders relaxed.
Take a deep breath and say your favorite affirmation aloud, with power:
"My No honors my truth."
"My energy is my responsibility."
"I release the need to please."
Feel your voice vibrate through your body — a reminder that your truth has sound.

6. Seal the Energy

Mist your aura with TrueJoy Empower Mist (bergamot + mint + sage).
Whisper: "My voice is clear. My boundaries are love."
Sit in silence for one minute — resting in the peace that follows self-honoring choice.

Journaling

Expressing Your Authentic Voice with Clarity and Grace

Intention

Your voice is an instrument of truth — not just for others, but for yourself.
Speaking truthfully aligns your inner and outer worlds.
This ritual helps you activate that integrity and clarity, turning
communication into connection.

"My truth is my power, spoken with love."

Mantra of the Ritual

"My words carry light.
My truth creates peace.
I speak with love and integrity."

Optional Enhancements

Perform before recording, presenting, or difficult conversations.
Use blue crystals like lapis lazuli or aquamarine to balance expression.
Chant or tone the sound "HAM" (throat chakra frequency).

Healing Integration

Speaking your truth doesn't create separation — it creates alignment.
When you use your voice consciously, your energy harmonizes with your purpose.
You stop trying to be understood and begin to radiate understanding.

"My truth isn't meant to convince — it's meant to express."

Expressing Your Authentic Voice with Clarity and Grace

The Ritual: Speaking From Heart and Clarity

1. Light the Truth Flame

Light your TrueJoy Voice Candle (eucalyptus + peppermint + jasmine).
Watch the flame flicker with vibrancy and whisper: "May my words carry light, not fear."
Inhale the cool, fresh scent and feel your chest open.
Healing Note: Eucalyptus clears mental fog, peppermint energizes focus, and jasmine inspires honest, heart-centered expression.

2. Anoint for Expression

Apply TrueJoy Voice Oil (blue chamomile + lemon + frankincense) to your throat, wrists, and heart.
Whisper: "I speak clearly. I speak kindly. I speak from truth."
Take three deep breaths, exhaling through the mouth with a soft "ahhh" sound — freeing the throat chakra.
Ancient Wisdom: Egyptian and Indian mystics considered the voice a divine tool — the bridge between heaven and Earth — where words create energy.

3. Breath of Clarity

Inhale through the nose for 4 counts, feeling your ribs expand.
Exhale slowly for 6 counts, releasing tightness in your jaw and throat.
Whisper: "I exhale fear. I inhale truth."
Repeat for 3–5 minutes until calm and clear.
Science Meets Soul: Conscious breathing relaxes the vagus nerve, improving tone and confidence in speech, while reducing the stress response before speaking difficult truths.

4. The Truth Activation Practice

Take your Journal and write:
Where have I silenced myself out of fear or people-pleasing?
What truth have I been holding back that wants to be expressed?
How can I speak this truth with love instead of defense?
Then write an Affirmative Declaration: "I trust my voice. I am worthy of being heard."
Healing Note: Writing activates the same neural pathways as speaking — preparing the subconscious mind to express with ease.

5. Voice Alignment Exercise

Sit upright, spine tall.
Inhale deeply, then exhale while humming softly — feeling vibration through your throat and chest.
Place your hand on your throat and whisper your affirmation aloud:
"My voice is powerful, steady, and true."
Repeat 3–5 times, allowing the words to resonate.

6. Seal the Energy

Mist your aura with TrueJoy Clarity Mist (lemongrass + lavender + mint).
Whisper: "I speak truth, I listen deeply, I communicate with love."
Stand tall and smile slightly — a soft embodiment of confidence and authenticity.

Journaling

(Use this space to write, draw, or simply breathe into the lessons of today's ritual.
There is no right or wrong — only what your soul needs to express.)

Shielding, Purifying, and Empowering Your Energy Field

Intention

Your aura — your energetic field — is your spiritual boundary.
It reflects your emotions, thoughts, and health.
This ritual strengthens your energy body so that you remain clear, calm, and
connected no matter what's happening around you.

"I am surrounded by light. My energy is safe, strong, and sovereign."

Mantra of the Ritual

"My light protects me.
My energy is clear and strong.
I move through the world surrounded by love."

Optional Enhancements

Place selenite or obsidian crystals near your workspace or bedside.
Perform under the waning moon to release heavy energy.
End with a salt bath or dry brushing ritual for physical cleansing.

Healing Integration

Energetic protection is not about fear — it's about alignment.
When you care for your energy, you operate from clarity, compassion, and inner
peace instead of reaction.
This ritual reminds you: your light is sacred — tend to it daily.

"Protection is not armor; it is awareness."

Shielding, Purifying, and Empowering Your Energy Field

The Ritual: Cleansing and Shielding Your Energy Field

1. Light the Protection Flame

Light your TrueJoy Energy Armor Candle (white sage + rosemary + frankincense).

Whisper: "As this flame burns, my energy becomes light and clear."

Watch the smoke rise and imagine it cleansing your space.

Healing Note: Sage purifies energy, rosemary boosts vitality, and frankincense seals your aura with divine protection.

2. Anoint for Strength

Apply TrueJoy Shield Oil (cypress + vetiver + black pepper) to your wrists, shoulders, and soles of your feet.

Whisper: "I am protected and grounded in light."

Visualize your energy forming a golden-white light around your entire body.

Ancient Wisdom: Ancient priests and shamans used plant-based oils to fortify their energetic field before rituals — believing aroma anchored spiritual armor in the body.

3. Smudge or Sound Cleanse

Choose your preferred cleansing method:

Smoke Cleanse: Use sage, cedar, or palo santo. Move clockwise around your body, saying: "All energy that is not mine returns to Source."

Sound Cleanse: Ring a bell or use a singing bowl three times, imagining vibration clearing stagnant energy.

Science Meets Soul: Sound frequencies break up stagnant energy and recalibrate the electromagnetic field surrounding the body — creating energetic coherence.

4. Visualization: The Golden Shield

Close your eyes and visualize a golden sphere of light surrounding you — about three feet in all directions.

Whisper: "This light is love. This light protects and renews me."

Imagine the sphere pulsing with warmth — porous enough to let love in, strong enough to keep negativity out.

Healing Note: Visualization activates the brain's reticular activating system, training your subconscious to maintain strong energetic boundaries.

5. Journal of Strength

In your Journal, write:

Where do I feel most energetically open or vulnerable? What situations or people drain my light?

How can I nurture my energy daily?

End your reflection with this statement: "My energy is my responsibility — and my greatest strength."

6. Seal the Aura

Mist your aura with TrueJoy Aura Mist (lemongrass + sandalwood + lavender).

Whisper: "I am light, I am grounded, I am safe."

Stand for one minute in silence, feeling peace radiating through your entire being.

Journaling

(Use this space to write, draw, or simply breathe into the lessons of today's ritual.
There is no right or wrong — only what your soul needs to express.)

Leading From Presence, Not Pressure

Intention

Power is not in volume — it's in vibration.
This ritual helps you cultivate energetic leadership by mastering calm authority:
the ability to stay centered, composed, and grounded no matter the environment.

"I don't chase power. I embody it."

Mantra of the Ritual

"My presence speaks louder than words.
My stillness is strength.
My calm creates trust."

Optional Enhancements

Perform barefoot to deepen grounding.
Play soft instrumental or cello music (432Hz for balance).
Place your hand on your solar plexus during meditation to
strengthen personal power.

Healing Integration

Calm authority is the divine union of power and peace.
When you lead from grounded energy, you naturally influence others through
presence rather than persuasion.
This ritual reminds you that embodied power doesn't control — it inspires.

"The most powerful person is the one who doesn't need to prove it."

Leading From Presence, Not Pressure
The Ritual: Cultivating Grounded Presence
1. Light the Authority Flame

Light your TrueJoy Presence Candle (amber + vetiver + sandalwood).
Watch the flame steady itself and whisper: "May my presence be calm, clear, and commanding."
Inhale the grounding scent and feel your energy begin to settle.
Healing Note: Vetiver roots the nervous system, amber stabilizes emotion, and sandalwood anchors your energy into the Earth — the essence of calm authority.

2. Anoint for Power

Apply TrueJoy Authority Oil (ginger + cedarwood + bergamot) to your wrists and over your solar plexus.
Whisper: "My confidence is quiet, my power is grounded."
Breathe deeply, visualizing golden light radiating from your core — the seat of personal power.
Ancient Wisdom: In Ayurveda, the solar plexus (Manipura chakra) governs strength and willpower. When balanced, it allows decisive yet compassionate leadership.

3. Grounding Meditation: The Still Mountain

Sit upright, feet flat on the floor.
Visualize yourself as a mountain — solid, ancient, unshakable.
Inhale deeply from the base up to your crown; exhale gently, releasing tension.
Whisper: "I am steady. I am strength. I am here."
Repeat for 5–7 minutes, feeling weight and stability in your presence.
Science Meets Soul: Grounding visualizations strengthen parasympathetic dominance — the physiological foundation of calm leadership under pressure.

4. Posture of Power

Stand tall, feet hip-width apart. Roll shoulders back and down, elongate your spine.
Bring hands to your sides, palms forward — a gesture of open authority.
Whisper: "I am the calm center of every storm."
Hold for 1–2 minutes, breathing slowly.
Feel the quiet force of your energy expand.
Healing Note: This posture signals confidence to your subconscious and communicates safety to others — the essence of embodied leadership.

5. Journal of Leadership

In your Journal, write: What does calm power feel like in my body?
Where do I overextend or overcontrol?
How can I lead with grounded presence today?
Then write your declaration: "I lead from peace, not pressure. My power serves love."

6. Seal the Energy

Mist your aura with TrueJoy Presence Mist (cypress + citrus + neroli). Whisper: "My calm is my command."
Stand still for a few moments — smile gently — and carry that composure into your day.

Journaling

(Use this space to write, draw, or simply breathe into the lessons of today's ritual.
There is no right or wrong — only what your soul needs to express.)

Reclaiming Strength Through Restoration and Self-Nurturing

Intention

Rest is not weakness — it is wisdom.
This ritual helps you shift from doing to being, reminding you that the true warrior honors their limits as sacred.
Stillness restores your energy, clears your mind, and reopens your heart to divine flow.

"I rest not because I am tired, but because I am wise."

Mantra of the Ritual

"I rest to remember my strength.
I pause to hear my wisdom.
I am restored in stillness."

Optional Enhancements

Add soft instrumental or nature sounds during rest.
Take a warm bath with Epsom salts and rose petals before or after.
Wear cozy, natural fabrics that feel nurturing to your skin.

Healing Integration

Rest is the root of resilience.
This ritual helps you refill your energetic reserves, realign your body's rhythm, and remember that surrender is a strength — not a surrendering of power, but a return to it.

"Even the warrior must lay down their sword to sharpen it."

Reclaiming Strength Through Restoration and Self-Nurturing

The Ritual: Returning to Power Through Peace

1. Light the Rest Flame

Light your TrueJoy Serenity Candle (lavender + chamomile + vanilla).
Watch the flame soften and whisper: "I surrender to stillness. My rest restores me."
Allow your body to exhale fully — signaling the mind that it is safe to relax.
Healing Note: Lavender calms the nervous system, chamomile soothes emotional stress, and vanilla creates a sense of safety and warmth.

2. Anoint for Release

Apply TrueJoy Restore Oil (clary sage + sandalwood + rose) to your temples, chest, and soles of your feet.
Whisper: "I release the need to strive. I am enough as I am."
Inhale slowly and imagine tension melting from your shoulders and jaw.
Ancient Wisdom: In Greek and Ayurvedic traditions, sacred oils were applied to the feet to ground spirit into body — reminding the warrior that power flows best through rest.

3. The Stillness Practice

Lie or sit comfortably with a blanket or shawl.
Close your eyes and take three deep breaths.
With each exhale, imagine the word release echoing softly through your body.
Whisper: "I return to myself."
Let your breath slow naturally and stay here for 10–15 minutes — no goal, just presence.
Science Meets Soul: Rest activates the parasympathetic ("rest and restore") system, reducing cortisol and improving cellular repair — literally rebuilding strength.

4. Gentle Heart Meditation

Place one hand on your heart and one on your belly.
Feel the rise and fall of your breath.
Silently say: "I am safe. I am held. I am home."
Stay here for as long as needed — allowing peace to wash through every cell.
Healing Note: This position regulates the vagus nerve, fostering a sense of internal calm and emotional safety — essential for long-term resilience.

5. Journal of Restoration

In your Journal, reflect: Where in my life am I pushing instead of allowing?
How does rest make me feel — guilt, fear, or relief?
What rituals bring me back to peace and replenishment?
Then write your declaration: "My rest fuels my rise. My stillness is my strength."

6. Seal the Energy

Mist your aura with TrueJoy Restore Mist (neroli + sandalwood + lavender).
Whisper: "I am replenished. I am whole. I am peace."
Sit quietly for one final moment, absorbing your own light.

Journaling

(Use this space to write, draw, or simply breathe into the lessons of today's ritual.
There is no right or wrong — only what your soul needs to express.)

Awakening to the Sacred in the Everyday

Intention

Each day is an initiation into life itself.
When you awaken with reverence, you align with grace — body, mind, and spirit in harmony.
This ritual helps you enter your day as ceremony — grounded, radiant, and fully present.

"Every sunrise is a new chance to live with love."

Mantra of the Ritual

"My morning is sacred.
My breath is prayer.
My presence is my power."

Optional Enhancements

Keep your phone on airplane mode for the first hour of your day.
Open curtains mindfully and say, "Welcome, light."
Play gentle acoustic or ambient music while you prepare for the day.
Use your TrueJoy Wholeness Tea Blend (lavender, lemon balm, rose) as your
mindful morning drink.

Healing Integration

Presence turns the ordinary into the divine.
When you begin your morning as ceremony, you create a rhythm of awareness
that ripples through every action that follows.
You no longer chase your day — you lead it with love.

"The way you greet the morning is the way you greet your life."

Awakening to the Sacred in the Everyday
The Ritual: Making Morning Sacred
1. Light the Dawn Flame

Light your TrueJoy Morning Presence Candle (orange blossom + cedar + white tea).
Whisper: "I awaken in gratitude. This day is sacred." As you breathe in the gentle aroma, let your heart open to the day ahead.
Healing Note: Orange blossom awakens joy, cedar centers the mind, and white tea purifies energy for a clear, grounded start.

2. Anoint for Presence

Apply TrueJoy Morning Oil (sweet orange + frankincense + rosemary) to your temples and wrists.
Whisper: "May my thoughts be clear, my actions be kind, and my presence be full."
Take a slow breath in and visualize golden light expanding through your body.
Ancient Wisdom: In Ayurvedic practice, morning abhyanga (self-anointing with oils) was used to seal the energy body and awaken the senses for clarity and vitality.

3. Gratitude Pouring Ritual

Pour yourself warm lemon water, tea, or your favorite morning drink into a special mug or cup.
Before sipping, pause and whisper: "This moment nourishes me. I receive the day with love."
Drink slowly, feeling gratitude for warmth, breath, and life itself.
Science Meets Soul: Starting the morning with gratitude activates serotonin and dopamine — training your mind for optimism and resilience.

4. Presence Meditation

Sit comfortably with eyes closed.
Breathe in for 4 counts, hold for 2, exhale for 6.
With each breath, silently say: "Inhale: I am here. Exhale: I am home."
Continue for 5–7 minutes, allowing awareness to fill your body like sunlight.
Healing Note: This rhythm balances the parasympathetic system, creating mental calm and alertness — the ideal state for presence.

5. Journal of Ceremony

In your Journal, write:
One thing I am grateful for today: _____
One way I can embody love today: _____
One intention for my energy today: _____
Then whisper your affirmation: "I enter this day with grace, presence, and joy."

6. Seal the Energy

Mist your aura or space with TrueJoy Morning Mist (lemon + peppermint + neroli).
Whisper: "I am awake. I am alive. I am aligned."
Smile softly — and begin your day with ceremony, not rush.

Journaling

(Use this space to write, draw, or simply breathe into the lessons of today's ritual. There is no right or wrong — only what your soul needs to express.)

Freeing Emotion, Reclaiming Joy, and Flowing with the Universe

Intention

Movement is meditation in motion.
When you dance consciously — not to perform, but to connect — your body
becomes the bridge between your soul and the physical world.
This ritual helps you awaken your life force, express emotions, and embody joy
through the sacred act of movement.

"I flow with life. I dance with grace. I move as love."

Mantra of the Ritual

"I am fluid like water.
I am free like air.
I am grounded like Earth.
I am light like fire."

Optional Enhancements

Dance barefoot outdoors or on natural ground to enhance grounding and freedom.
Use your TrueJoy Harmony Oil after movement to balance energy centers.
End with herbal tea — ginger or tulsi — to settle the nervous system.
Create a personal playlist called "The Rhythm of My Soul."

Healing Integration

This ritual teaches that your body is your greatest teacher.
When you listen, it tells you when to move, when to rest, and how to
return to balance.
Through sacred movement, you don't escape your emotions — you alchemize them
into flow, freedom, and love.
"When you move with intention, you become the dance."

Freeing Emotion, Reclaiming Joy, and Flowing with the Universe

The Ritual: Awakening Through Movement

1. Light the Movement Flame

Light your TrueJoy Flow Candle (jasmine + sandalwood + grapefruit).Whisper: "I open to the rhythm of life within me."
Watch the flame flicker — feel your own inner spark awakening.
Healing Note: Jasmine elevates mood and sensuality, sandalwood grounds awareness, and grapefruit activates energy and joy.

2. Anoint for Flow

Apply TrueJoy Flow Oil (lemongrass + rose + bergamot) to your wrists, chest, and ankles.
Whisper: "I release control. I trust my body's wisdom."
Take three deep breaths, inviting energy to rise from your feet upward.
Ancient Wisdom: In ancient temple dances from Egypt to India, movement was prayer — a way to communicate with spirit and realign the body's energy centers.

3. Awakening Movement Meditation

Begin standing tall, feet grounded. Roll your shoulders back and gently sway side to side.
Inhale as your arms lift upward; exhale as they flow down. Whisper: "I am the breath in motion."
Let your movements become natural — intuitive, unplanned.
Move for 10–15 minutes with music that feels expansive and alive (try 528Hz, tribal drums, or ambient flow).
Science Meets Soul: Free-form movement reduces stress hormones and increases endorphins and dopamine — literally changing your mood and energy state.

4. Emotional Expression Flow

As you move, notice emotions rising — joy, sadness, gratitude, release.
Allow them to move through you, not stay in you.
Whisper as you exhale: "I am safe to feel. I am safe to release."
Healing Note: Movement gives emotion permission to flow, releasing stored energy from the hips, chest, and heart. The more you let go, the lighter your spirit becomes.

5. Stillness & Integration

When the movement naturally slows, place your hands on your heart.
Close your eyes and whisper: "Thank you, body, for carrying me."
Stand in stillness for 3–5 minutes, feeling the pulse of life within you.
Breathe. Smile. Be.

6. Journal of Flow

In your Journal, write: What emotions surfaced during my movement?
Where did I feel the most flow or resistance?
How can I bring this openness into my day?
Then affirm: "I move through life with freedom and joy."

7. Seal the Energy

Mist your aura with TrueJoy Flow Mist (orange blossom + patchouli + mint).
Whisper: "I move with the rhythm of the universe." Let yourself sway once more — one last dance of gratitude.

Journaling

(Use this space to write, draw, or simply breathe into the lessons of today's ritual. There is no right or wrong — only what your soul needs to express.)

Honoring the Body, Blessing the Food, and Receiving with Grace

Intention

Food is love made visible.
When you eat with awareness, you don't just feed the body — you feed your spirit.
This ritual reminds you that nourishment is sacred, pleasure is holy, and receiving care (even from yourself) is an act of devotion.
"Every bite I take is an affirmation of love."

Mantra of the Ritual

"My body is my temple.
My meals are my prayers.
I am nourished in every way."

Optional Enhancements

Use your TrueJoy Grounding Tea or Calm Digestive Blend before eating.
Eat in silence or with gentle music to amplify sensory connection.
Use intentional plating — natural wood, ceramic, or stone to connect to the Earth element.
Take one mindful bite with your eyes closed to experience pure presence.

Healing Integration

Eating consciously reconnects you to the rhythm of life.
It transforms consumption into communion — a moment of remembrance that your body is divine, your nourishment is sacred, and love flows through everything you receive.

"When you eat with love, you feed your soul."

Honoring the Body, Blessing the Food, and Receiving with Grace

The Ritual: Eating as Ceremony

1. Prepare with Intention

Before cooking or eating, light your TrueJoy Nourish Candle (cinnamon + orange + vanilla).
Whisper: "May this food bless my body, mind, and heart."
Feel gratitude for every hand that helped bring your meal to life — the farmers, the sun, the soil, the rain.
Healing Note: Cinnamon awakens warmth and joy, orange uplifts mood, and vanilla calms the nervous system — inviting peace into your meal space.

2. Anoint for Gratitude

Dab a small drop of TrueJoy Nourish Oil (cardamom + clove + rose) on your wrists or over your heart.
Whisper: "I receive nourishment with love and presence."
Take one deep breath, feeling your body open to receive — not just food, but care and abundance.
Ancient Wisdom: In many sacred traditions, oil anointing before a meal signified purification and receptivity — the body prepared as a temple for divine nourishment.

3. Bless the Food

Sit with your meal before you. Place your hands over the plate or bowl.
Whisper softly: "May this food restore my energy, elevate my spirit, and remind me of the sacredness of life."
Pause and notice the colors, aromas, and textures — awakening your senses before the first bite.
Science Meets Soul: Engaging all five senses before eating activates the parasympathetic ("rest and digest") system, improving digestion and nutrient absorption.

4. Eat with Awareness

Take your first bite slowly. Chew fully, breathing deeply between bites. Notice flavors, temperature, texture.
Whisper internally: "This food is love becoming energy."
Put down your utensils between bites — letting your body lead your pace.
Healing Note: Mindful eating balances the gut-brain axis, calms stress hormones, and creates emotional satisfaction, reducing the urge to overconsume.

5. Gratitude Pause

When you're halfway through your meal, pause. Take a sip of water or tea, and whisper:
"I honor this moment of receiving."
Feel your heart expand — this is the intersection of nourishment and gratitude.

6. Completion of Grace

As you finish, bring your hands to your heart and close your eyes.
Whisper: "Thank you, body, for receiving. Thank you, Earth, for giving."
Sit for one minute in silence, letting gratitude digest alongside your meal.

7. Journal of Nourishment

In your Journal, write: How did it feel to eat slowly and intentionally?
Did I notice any emotions arise while receiving nourishment?
What am I truly hungry for — body, heart, or soul?
Then write your closing affirmation: "I am nourished by love in all forms."

Journaling

(Use this space to write, draw, or simply breathe into the lessons of today's ritual.
There is no right or wrong — only what your soul needs to express.)

Restoring, Releasing, and Reconnecting at Day's End

Intention

As the day closes, you are invited to slow, soften, and surrender.
Evening Radiance transforms your bedtime into a sacred ceremony — a return
to your inner sanctuary.
"As I rest, I renew. As I release, I rise."

Mantra of the Ritual

"I rest deeply.
I release completely.
I awaken renewed."

Optional Enhancements

Keep a crystal like amethyst or moonstone beside your bed for soothing energy.
Brew TrueJoy Sleep Tea (lavender, chamomile, rose).
Play 432Hz frequency music or nature sounds.
Use natural fabrics (cotton, linen, silk) for your bedding — symbolic
of softness and surrender.

Healing Integration

Rest is the sacred reset of life.
In this ritual, you remember that rest is not retreat — it's the rebuilding of
your radiance. When you surrender to stillness, your body repairs, your mind resets,
and your soul whispers its wisdom.

"The light of your day depends on how gently you let the night hold you."

Restoring, Releasing, and Reconnecting at Day's End

The Ritual: Returning to Stillness

1. Light the Radiance Flame

Light your TrueJoy Evening Radiance Candle (lavender + sandalwood + ylang-ylang).

Whisper: "I release this day with gratitude and grace."

Watch the flame glow gently, symbolizing your transition from activity to peace.

Healing Note: Lavender soothes the mind, sandalwood grounds the body, and ylang-ylang balances emotions — creating the chemistry of calm.

2. Anoint for Release

Apply TrueJoy Radiance Oil (chamomile + cedarwood + vanilla) to your temples, chest, and soles of your feet.

Whisper: "I let go of what is complete. I invite peace to take its place."

Take three deep breaths, feeling tension dissolve from your body.

Ancient Wisdom: Egyptian priestesses anointed the body before rest to signify divine protection during sleep — believing dreams were messages from the soul.

3. Gentle Release Movement

Roll your shoulders, stretch your spine, and take slow, circular movements with your wrists and ankles.

Inhale through the nose, exhale through the mouth with a sigh.

Whisper: "I soften into stillness." Let the movements grow slower until you naturally settle.

Science Meets Soul: Slow rhythmic movement before rest signals safety to the nervous system, lowering cortisol and preparing the body for deep sleep.

4. Evening Reflection Meditation

Sit or lie comfortably. Place your right hand on your heart and left on your belly.

Breathe deeply and reflect: What moments today brought me joy?

What do I choose to release?

What am I grateful for right now?

Whisper: "I am thankful. I am peaceful. I am home."

Healing Note: This reflection ritual rewires the brain toward gratitude — reducing rumination and promoting restful sleep.

5. Journal of Radiance

In your Journal, write: Three things I'm grateful for today

One thing I learned

One thing I release before rest

Then affirm: "I rest in the glow of gratitude."

6. Sacred Rest Preparation

Mist your pillow and aura with TrueJoy Dream Mist (lavender + clary sage + rose).

Whisper: "I rest in peace. I awaken in light."

Dim the lights, silence your phone, and let stillness surround you.

Take three deep breaths — and surrender to rest.

Journaling

(Use this space to write, draw, or simply breathe into the lessons of today's ritual. There is no right or wrong — only what your soul needs to express.)

Allowing Love, Abundance, and Guidance to Flow Freely

Intention

Receiving is an act of trust — a declaration that you are worthy of care, ease, and divine support. This ritual helps you clear blocks around receiving and open your energetic heart to the infinite flow that's already waiting to meet you.

"I open my heart to receive all that is meant for me — with ease, grace, and gratitude."

Mantra of the Ritual

"I am open.
I am deserving.
I am supported."

Optional Enhancements

Perform this ritual under a waxing moon to amplify abundance energy.
Place rose quartz or citrine on your heart while meditating.
Listen to 528Hz or "Weightless" by Marconi Union for energetic softening.
End with herbal tea — rose, tulsi, or chamomile — to support gentle receptivity.

Healing Integration

Receiving is an energetic mirror: the way you receive reflects how deeply you trust life.
This ritual rewires scarcity into openness — replacing "I must do" with "I allow."
Through receiving, you complete the circle of giving and return to the natural balance of flow.

"What you seek is also seeking you — but it cannot reach you until you open the door."

Allowing Love, Abundance, and Guidance to Flow Freely

The Ritual: From Resistance to Receptivity

1. Light the Flow Flame

Light your TrueJoy Receive Candle (rose + vanilla + jasmine).
Whisper: "I open to the abundance and love that surround me."
Watch the flame as it steadies — a reflection of your open yet grounded energy.
Healing Note: Rose activates the heart, jasmine inspires openness, and vanilla invites sweetness — softening the body's subtle defenses against receiving.

2. Anoint for Openness

Apply TrueJoy Receive Oil (ylang-ylang + neroli + cedarwood) to your heart, palms, and wrists.
Whisper: "I am safe to receive. I am worthy to receive."
Place your hands over your heart, feeling its rhythm — your body's reminder that you are always being given to.
Ancient Wisdom: In Taoist and tantric traditions, the art of receiving was seen as active surrender — not passive waiting, but conscious openness to the divine flow of life.

3. Heart Opening Breath

Sit comfortably with shoulders relaxed. Inhale deeply through your heart space, expanding the chest.
Exhale through your mouth with a sigh, releasing tension.
Repeat for 7 cycles, whispering: "Inhale love. Exhale resistance."
Science Meets Soul: Heart-focused breathing increases coherence between the brain and heart, opening emotional receptivity and aligning body and mind with trust.

4. Receiving Visualization

Close your eyes and imagine a golden waterfall of light cascading over you.
This light carries abundance, healing, love, and ease.
Whisper: "I am open to receive."
Visualize your cells drinking in this golden light — your whole being illuminated by divine nourishment.
Healing Note: Visualization helps the subconscious reprogram the nervous system to expect safety and support, replacing scarcity with flow.

5. Gratitude Activation

In your Journal, write: 3 ways I am supported right now (seen or unseen). 1 thing I'm willing to receive today. 1 way I can allow ease instead of controlThen affirm:"Everything I desire is already moving toward me. I receive with gratitude."

6. Receiving Gesture

Stand tall, arms open wide, palms facing the sky. Whisper: "I receive with joy."
Take a slow breath in, imagining energy flowing from the universe into your hands
and down into your heart. Exhale, whisper: "Thank you." Repeat 3 times.

7. Seal the Energy

Mist your aura with TrueJoy Flow Mist (orange blossom + patchouli + mint).
Whisper: "The universe gives freely, and I receive fully."
Smile softly, hand on heart — the gesture of complete receptivity.

Journaling

(Use this space to write, draw, or simply breathe into the lessons of today's ritual. There is no right or wrong — only what your soul needs to express.)

CLOSING CEREMONY —
THE FULL CIRCLE OF EMBODIMENT

Honoring the Journey, Integrating the Lessons, and Living as TrueJoy

You began this journey seeking grounding, healing, and direction — and through each pillar,
you've become the embodiment of your own light.
Now, in this final ceremony, you don't just complete the path — you become it.
This moment is not an ending; it's an awakening to a new rhythm —
one guided by love, trust, and alignment.
"Transformation was never about becoming something new —
it was about remembering who you've always been."

Mantra of the Ritual

"I am the ritual.
I am the lesson.
I am the love that moves through all things."

Optional Enhancements

Perform under the full moon or at sunrise — the thresholds of renewal.
Create a small altar with symbols from each pillar (stone, flower, feather,
candle, journal, cup).
Play soft harp or Tibetan bowl music (528Hz or 963Hz).
End with tea or cacao as a "communion of joy."

Healing Integration

This is your return home — not to the beginning, but to your essence.
You now carry the energy of TrueJoy in every breath, every thought, every
moment of being. Your daily life is the ritual.
*"You are the flame that cannot be extinguished —
you are the light you were always seeking."*

The Ceremony of Embodiment

1. Light the Circle Flame

Light your TrueJoy Completion Candle (myrrh + sandalwood + rose).
Whisper: "As I light this flame, I honor the journey that shaped me."
Watch the flame and feel gratitude for every step — the dark nights, the
breakthroughs, the
quiet moments of courage.

*Healing Note: Myrrh represents closure and reverence; sandalwood symbolizes
wisdom;*
rose opens the heart to gratitude.

2. Anoint for Wholeness

Apply TrueJoy Wholeness Oil (frankincense + jasmine + cedarwood) to your heart,
temples, and wrists.
Whisper: "All parts of me are welcome here. I am whole."
Feel your energy unify — mind, body, spirit — merging in harmony.

*Ancient Wisdom: Many indigenous traditions used sacred oils during rites of passage to
signify integration*
— the spirit fully returning home to the body.

3. The Circle of Gratitude

Place your hand on your heart and whisper gratitude for: The version of you who began this journey.
The lessons that shaped your strength. The divine rhythm that brought you here.
"Thank you, body, for carrying me.
Thank you, mind, for learning.
Thank you, heart, for loving.
Thank you, spirit, for guiding."

Healing Note: Gratitude activates the vibration of completion — closing the loop of creation and
anchoring joy into the nervous system.

4. Candle of Continuation

As your candle burns, take one final journal reflection:
What truth do I now live by?
What am I ready to share with the world?
How will I continue to embody TrueJoy each day?

Then, write your final affirmation — your declaration of embodiment:
"I am not becoming — I am being.
I live as light.
I am TrueJoy."
When ready, blow out the candle softly, saying:

"The flame remains within me."

Thank You

"Every time you light a candle, take a breath, or open your heart —
you remind the world what peace feels like."

Thank you for walking this journey with me.
May these rituals bring you back to yourself —
to the steady rhythm
beneath the noise, to the quiet wisdom within your breath,
and to the love that has always lived inside you.
You are the living expression of TrueJoy — grounded, awakened,
radiant, and whole.
If these practices have inspired you, continue to explore the
TrueJoy Living experience through our community, retreats, and
spa line — each created to help you live your ritual every day.
Keep lighting your candle. Keep coming home.

With love and gratitude,
Joy Hafner
Founder, TrueJoy Living
www.TrueJoy-Living.com